The Ultimate Parenting Guide

How to Enjoy Peaceful Parenting and Joyful Children

Yong Hui V. McDonald

"Chaplain Yong Hui McDonald hit a home run with this book. We all need more wisdom on how to raise our children and how to let go and forgive those who have hurt us in our childhood."

— Angela McMahan, President/CEO, Arising Hope (Faith Based Domestic Violence Shelter in Colorado)

"Anything can happen as we grow through the stages of adolescence to adulthood. Expectations of our parents are usually only of nurtured love. Chaplain McDonald tells the story of being pulled in both emotional directions. One of unconditional love by her mother. And one of mental and physical abuse by her father. Because of the vivid actions of our parents, children can follow suit in either a positive or negative persuasion. Chaplain McDonald has overcome multiple tragedies in her life. The inspiration that comes across in her books depicts her great faith and devotion. Her driving force is the healing power of the Holy Spirit.

— Robert H. Garcia, AT&T Engineer, retired, Thornton, Colorado, current inmate and follower of the Word of God.

THE ULTIMATE PARENTING GUIDE
How to Enjoy Peaceful Parenting and Joyful Children

Books, audio books, DVDs written and produced by Yong Hui V. McDonald are also available. To purchase, contact www.griefpathway.com or order by www.atlasbooks.com/ griefpathway, phone: 1-800-booklog or 1-800-266-5564.

GriefPathway Ventures LLC, P.O. Box 220, Brighton, CO 80601. Adora Productions is an imprint of the GriefPathway Ventures LLC. Website: www.griefpathway.com.
Email: griefpwv@gmail.com

Published by Adora Productions
Printed in the United States of America
ISBN: 978-1-935791-34-8
Cover Picture by Tara Rose, Traditions Photography
Cover Design by Lynette McClain
Cover Art & Design Copyright ©2011 Adora Productions
First Printing: August 2011

1. Parenting 2. Children 3. Spiritual Healing 4. Prayer
5. Christianity

CONTENTS

9. Teach them to be generous
10. Avoid favoritism
11. Treat your parents with love and respect
12. Teach them what it means to fear God
13. Teach them to manage their time
14. Teach them how to grieve their losses
15. Teach them how to forgive
16. Protect them from violent situations
17. Teach them good moral values
18. Be there for your children
19. Teach them to pray
20. Lead them to the Lord
21. Be their cheerleader
22. Teach them to love God more than money
23. Teach them to have a dream
24. Dedicate your children and find peace
25. Ask God for help with parenting
26. Ask for forgiveness when you make a mistake
27. Encourage them to get a higher education
28. Find godly mentors for your children
29. Encourage them to read good books
30. Don't repeat the mistakes your parents have made
31. Have a good relationship with your spouse
32. Teach them to listen to God's voice
33. Teach them about the spiritual battle
34. Teach them to love and worship Jesus
35. Teach them to find a spouse with high moral values.
36. Learn the lessons from Job about parenting
37. Teach them about humor and coping skills
38. Teach them to be self-sufficient
39. Take them on trips to build good memories
40. Proclaim victory for your children

DEDICATION

I dedicate this book to my loving heavenly Father, my Lord Jesus, and to the Holy Spirit. Also to my mother who has positively impacted my life more than anyone. She is a perfect gift from the Lord and I am blessed beyond measure because of her faith and love for the Lord and love for all her children.

ACKNOWLEDGMENTS

I thank God for my wonderful mother, for her love and prayers for me. I believe that because of her prayers the Lord has blessed me and my ministry beyond my imagination. I am deeply indebted to my wonderful husband Keith, who died in a car accident, and is with the Lord. He helped my ministry preparation more than anyone I've ever met. I also thank my beautiful children, Fletcher and Nicole. I pray that God will bless them beyond their imagination in all areas of life.

I thank all ACDF saints who contributed their stories and also those who edited this book: Dena Anderson, Kathleen Cooper, Mary Diubaldo, Patricia Dowson, Danielle Engstrom, Brittany Espinosa, Rita Finney, Robert Garcia, Felonis Hernandez, Nadia Garcia, Bobbi Ignasiak, Irva Lenzini, Russett Loucks, Heather Lopez, Amy Low, Tiffany Lobato, Lisa Newberry, Renea Pacheco, Arlene Pereda, Amanda Powers, Jennifer Richardson, Eli Sandoval, Cheryl Killion, Raelyn Santoya, Christina Sears, Juanita Tamayo, Lakiesha Vigil, Michelle Vigil, Mary Voogt, and Christine Ward. Also, I thank Diedra Duncan, Tina Love, Janet Lysko, Amy Penn, and Bobbi Ignasiak for helping me edit this book. I thank everyone who helped me with editing but their names are not listed here.

Finally, I give glory to Jesus. Without Him, this book could not have been written.

INTRODUCTION

HOW DID THIS BOOK COME ABOUT?

All my children are grown and have left home. I am thankful that I have a wonderful relationship with them, but I wish I had known what I know now about parenting 26 years ago, before they were born. I have learned some valuable lessons about parenting, but I had no plans to write a book; then God changed that.

On March 25, 2011, I was writing a book but it wasn't a parenting book. The Lord asked me to write a book to help parents based on my mother's story. At first, I wasn't sure if I could write a book on parenting. I felt I wasn't ready, but using my mother as an example made perfect sense to me.

My mother is 83 years old and has been my role model all of my life. She has been a blessing to all of her children. I am proud of her. I am grateful that God has given me a wonderful, godly mother.

Interestingly, when I visited my mother in Los Angeles, in 2010, the Holy Spirit asked me to write her story for the first time. I immediately got my laptop computer out and asked my mother if she had anything that she wanted to share about her life story.

She was delighted that I asked her about her life. She told me many amazing stories about how God has helped her in times of pain and struggles as well as joy. I didn't know why I had to type her stories at the time, but it has become clear to me now. He wanted to use her story to teach others about parenting.

While writing this book, the Lord opened my eyes and made me realize that He has helped me in my parenting. He wanted me to share it with other people so they can see how God can help them as well.

In addition, I have encountered many grieving

parents at Adams County Detention Facility (ACDF) because of their incarceration and separation from their children and the feeling of helplessness. Many people are in need of God's healing and guidance. God is the only one who can help them find peace, comfort and wisdom in the midst of impossible situations. Therefore, their stories of tears, pain, suffering and healing are also included in this book to tell others how God can help us in our pain and trials of parenting.

About a month into my writing, I gave thanks to God for asking me to write this book. I realized the importance of learning about parenting. I have encountered many people who have been hurt by their parents. There is a great need for reflection and processing pain for adult children in order to be a loving and nurturing parent. Healing from a broken heart is possible through God.

We as parents need to make intentional efforts to plant the seeds of faith in our children's hearts if we want to see good fruits someday. We need God's wisdom to raise our children. And this book gives you time to reflect and the areas you need to process so you can overcome pains caused by your parents. Also it gives you ideas as to which area you need to work on when you raise children.

Parenting does not stop until we die. We can continue to help our children even if we have made mistakes of our own. So, wherever you are, open up to the Lord's guidance so you will gain wisdom and healing and become the parent God wants you to be. He is willing to help us and that is what this book is about.

Chapter 1

Reflections on Parenting

1. The Storm

1. Troubles

My parents were born on the same day, in the same town, 15 miles apart, October 1, 1927, in Song Hwan, South Korea. My mother's father passed away when she was 16 years old, her older brother assumed the head of household for the family. My mother's home hosted a church where she grew up having great faith in God.

When she was 21 years old, an arrangement was made by my uncle for her to get married. She cried for three days and refused to eat anything and had expressed she would not marry a non-Christian.

My grandmother visited my paternal grandfather and said, "My son made a mistake and the wedding has to be canceled because my daughter will not marry a non-Christian."

"That wouldn't be a problem," My paternal grand-father said, "She can go to church and we don't oppose Christian belief."

So, my mother eventually married my father. When my grandmother was younger she had a miscarriage. She was bedridden and could not walk for seven years. My mother took care of her consistently. She took her to the doctor to church and prayed for her healing. Her prayers were answered and my grandmother was able to walk again. This was the time many problems came up.

My grandmother told my mother not to attend church anymore. Soon my father sided with my grandmother and told my mother not to attend church as well. My mother was in turmoil. She stopped attending church for a while to please them. My grandmother was not kind to her even after my mother stopped attending church. So, she decided to resume her attendance.

My father was drafted into the Korean Army in 1950. My father was shot in the leg during the war. The bullet missed the bone, but was stuck in his upper leg. The doctors had to dig the bullet out. My father was honorably discharged after recovery. Shortly after my father's discharge, my older brother was born. My brother was a colic child and cried a lot. My father who didn't like to hear a baby crying, hit him a lot. From the time I was born my father favored me because I smiled a lot. My sister Kyong Hui was born soon after.

My mother supported the family by sewing. After my grandfather passed away, my father didn't work, and was into gambling heavily. One day my mother caught him trying to take the sewing machine to get gambling money. She held on tightly to the sewing machine and didn't let go. My mother tried to convince my father to move to another town so he could find a job, but he refused. My mother, my older brother and my younger sister moved to Song Tan City where the American Air Force base was located. I stayed with my father and my grandmother for about six months. When my mother had settled down, my father finally agreed to move, so we went to live with the rest of the family. I was five years old when my father started his business. At that time my younger sister and brother were born.

2. Guidance

One of the good memories I had of my father was when my father came home and asked all three daughters to dance while he was eating dinner. He was so happy and pleased with us that he gave us money after we entertained him. During those times, his drinking was still under control and I thought our family was happy. When we were old enough to attend preschool, my mother had all of us attend church. My older brother dropped out of the church early on. My father and grandmother told him he didn't have to go to church.

I loved attending church. I sang in the children's choir. The songs I sang about Jesus helped me to grow in my faith. While growing up, I often wished that my parents would attend church together. I had a friend whose parents attended church together and they always looked very happy.

3. A Prisoner

Even though my father was gentle with his daughters, he was not kind to my older brother. One day my father was angry and he tied up my older brother's hands with wires, put him in a room and ordered the rest of the family not to give him any food. My brother was treated like a prisoner at home.

One day I overheard my father's conversation with my mother about how he took my older brother to the mountains in the dark one evening. He said he tied up my brother's hands and made him watch as he dug a hole. He told my brother that he was digging a hole to bury him. My brother managed to untie himself and ran away. My father couldn't see him in the darkness to catch him.

I couldn't believe what I heard. I had no idea how my brother must have felt about the world when his father treated him this way. While I was growing up, there were no laws against domestic violence. My brother's spirit was crushed as well as all of ours.

I don't know how my brother got back home but he did. I was very close to my older brother and he was very kind to me. At school, he was always there to protect me. At home, my brother was continually getting into trouble.

4. Prayer

I realized that my father had a drinking problem when his temper was out of control. When he wasn't drinking a lot, he was kind. I started praying to God to help my father quit drinking. I was in the fourth grade at the time and I was determined to keep praying. I thought if I prayed hard enough, God would help my father quit drinking.

I remembered the long walks from school and how hard I prayed for my father. When I came home, my mother would send me to find my father at the bars in order to bring him home. He would never come home with me. One day he finally had it, and he yelled at me telling me not to come and look for him anymore. I was very upset, but I felt relieved when my mother started sending my younger sisters to look for him at the bars. He always came home late at night drunk.

I kept praying, thinking that God would do something about my father's drinking. Then one day an understanding came to me. I believe it came from the Lord that my father would not quit drinking until he died. The fact I had to learn was that God would not make this decision for my father. He had to make the decision on his own. Strangely, I had peace when that understanding came to me. I knew what I needed to do. I had to stop praying for my father's drinking problem.

When I shared this with my grandmother, she misunderstood me and thought I wanted my father to die. I didn't realize this until the evening when my father was yelling at my mother saying that I wanted him to die. What a mistake! I should not have said anything at all to my grandmother.

5. Options

My mother's problems continued with her going to church. My father threatened her with a knife, but she told him she would rather die than quit going to church. Suddenly, my father started having problems breathing. He couldn't hold the knife anymore and he threw it down in frustration.

"I don't feel good," my father said.

My mother suggested, "You could go to Dae Chun and enjoy the sea or you could go to Sam Kak Mountain where people go on retreats."

He told her he would go to Sam Kak Mountain to see if he could become a believer. My mother made arrangements for him. My father, my grandmother, and I stayed on the mountain for sixteen days. We attended four worship services every day, this was when my father and my grandmother began to believe in God.

My father's breathing problems were completely gone when he returned home. My grandmother became supportive of my mother attending church after that. My father stopped drinking and smoking and attended church with the rest of the family. There was finally peace at home. Unfortunately, six months later he started drinking again and stopped attending church.

6. The Storm

One day, my father started beating on my mother. I remember seeing my brother running out the door. I was struggling to hold onto my father's arms trying to stop him from hitting my mother. My brother left home when he was 12 years old. He was homeless, was wandering the streets. He wasn't strong enough to protect our mother and he couldn't bear to watch our mother being beaten by our own father. There were no homeless shelters in the area for him to rely on.

My brother was involved in gangs and went to prison three times. I felt sorry for my brother. I believed that if my father would have provided a loving and nurturing environment, he would not have ran away and gotten into trouble with the law.

I suffered so much from watching the abuse and violence, that I struggled with hate and anger. I was in turmoil and I confronted my father's abusive behavior. He hated me for taking my brother and mother's side. He became critical of me and even criticized that I was too skinny. My father was slim and I had my father's figure but he didn't see it. I was my father's favorite child, but that was coming to an end.

7. Heavenly Father

There was no peace at home, only turmoil and fighting. I had a difficult time understanding how our Heavenly Father can be good, since my earthly father was a total failure to me. It took a long time for me to separate my earthly father from my Heavenly Father.

I desperately needed healing from the Lord. My daily prayer became, "God please forgive me. I cannot love my father. Help me to forgive him." But I couldn't do it when my father was continuously hitting my mother.

8. No Respect

My father seemed to have no respect for anyone anymore. My mother had two younger brothers who lived in our town. They were very nice and kind people. When my drunken father started yelling at them in their convenience store, they moved to a different town instead of fighting back. One of my uncles, who became a pastor, later visited our home and reconciled with my father.

My father wasn't happy with my paternal grand-mother either. Once, in a rage, he got up and grabbed the clock from the wall and threw it outside, shouting at his mother that the clock was all he would inherit from his parents. This happened in front of all of us. He was only thinking about what he should receive from his parents, and not what he could give them.

At the time, the oldest son in the family took care of their elderly parents. My father's two younger sisters were kind to their mother and they took care of her as well.

9. My Sister

My sister Kyong Hui was 18 years old when my father sent her off to work in Song Nam city. It was her senior year in high school, my father couldn't wait until she could make money to help him. While riding a bicycle, she was hit by a car, killing her instantly.

My sister and I were very close. I was in shock after her death. I was grieving deeply, depressed, bedridden and suffered nightmares and headaches. My mother would pray for me to heal. I experienced God's healing power through her prayer.

She told me to read the Bible. I started reading it. While reading Romans, God helped me realize that I was a sinner. I asked God in tears to forgive me. For the first time in my life, I experienced peace like I have never experienced before. God was real. I loved to read the Bible, so I decided to attend Suwon Bible College.

My mother also explained to me that there is a spiritual world. I didn't know anything about spiritual battle until she explained it to me. I was grieving from the loss of my sister and was vulnerable. The devil used this opportunity to attack me in my dreams and even when I was awake. My mother told me to pray and read the Bible so I could be strong and be freed from the devil's attacks. I followed my mother's suggestion, it helped me tremendously. It took a while but I was eventually healed from depression, anxiety, fear, worry and torment. I found peace and healing through God. I could have suffered a lot more emotionally, mentally and spiritually if my mother had not been there to pray for me and guide me.

My mother was gone a lot because she was helping at my father's business. Whenever she had the time, she took me to many revival meetings. She sent me to retreats in the mountains and to healing services held in different towns. Sometimes we visited a church in the mountains together so we could fast and get direction from the Lord. All of these different events and experiences have helped me to grow in my faith.

10. The Pain

My father was after my mother again with a knife and my mother was hiding at her brother's home next to ours. I told her to divorce our father, but she said she couldn't. I told her we could take care of ourselves. She said I could because I was older, but not my younger sister and brother.

One day she was hiding again, but this time in the attic while my father was ranting and raving because he couldn't find her. The next morning, she accidently fell from the attic, about ten feet, and she became unconscious. I told my father we needed to take her to the hospital, but he yelled at me and refused to take her to the hospital. I called my mother's pastor and he came with his wife. They convinced my father that my mother needed help. My mother was hospitalized for about two weeks. She hurt her neck from the accident and suffered pain and stiffness from thereon. It was a miracle that she survived.

11. The Price

My brother was in and out of the house during his teenage years. When he got a little older, he earned a black belt in Tae Kwon Do. My brother was my security. I always felt safe on the street because everyone knew him and his skills. He didn't believe in God, but when I went to church, he walked with me saying that he wanted me to be safe.

As I was growing up, I felt more love from my older brother than my parents. When he was at the bar no one could talk him into coming home, but he would listen to me and come home. He told me about life on the streets and what was happening out there with gangs and all.

My brother told me later on that he wasn't afraid of anyone, except our father. The situation changed after my older brother became bigger. My father couldn't beat him anymore. One day I was told that my brother was drunk and yelling at our father, I wasn't surprised. My brother carried lots of hurt and anger toward our father. Later, my father told me how my brother was threatening him and said, "You need to take care of me." My father ruled his family with disrespect and violence. My older brother started doing exactly the same except he never hit my father.

One evening, I saw my older brother drunk, walking towards my father's room. I sensed that it wasn't going to be a good scene if he saw our father. I stopped my brother and told him that he should be kind to our father. He listened to me and went to his room to sleep.

A bitter seed had been planted in my older brother's heart, and my father was seeing the fruit of it. I wondered what would have happened if my father had treated his family with love and respect. Our family could have been living in peace, and we could have loved and respected each other, but the damage had already been done.

My father never hit me, but I grieved over all the hurts and damage he did to my older brother, my mother and the family. When my brother moved out, that was a relief for all of us because of his grief.

12. Lessons

My father taught me two very important lessons. One is don't drink alcohol and two is don't lose your temper. Otherwise everyone around you, especially your family suffers greatly. I don't touch alcohol. I don't want to take any chances of hurting myself and others. I have seen the destructiveness, devastation and embarrassment which is caused by alcoholism.

I felt so embarrassed in my sixth grade year when other students described how my drunken father couldn't even stand and walk straight on the street. I wanted to hide from everyone when I heard that.

The other lesson is don't marry a non-believer if you are a Christian. What my mother had gone through because she had faith in God was not going to happen to me. I decided to marry a Christian who doesn't drink alcohol. I am thankful that God helped me to find a husband who met this important criteria.

13. The Loss

My father's story is really sad at the end. Our family suffered a lot from our father's abusive behavior until he committed suicide in 1978, one-and-a-half months after I got married. He was drunk when he killed himself. This was the worst thing that happened to my family. After all of the abuse, there was no time to reconcile with each other. He was gone forever. I was so angry after he left a note saying, "Wife is useless, children are useless." I tore the paper and threw it in the garbage. I struggled with many issues caused by my father, but God started healing my heart by helping me understand my father's love on the way to the grave. That was the beginning of my healing journey which took many years to come.

14. Mother's Struggle

My parents had financial problems before my father took his own life. They tried to sell the house but were unable. Right after my father's death, my mother fasted three days and asked God to help her sell the house so she could take care of the debt. God answered her prayers. Right after the fasting, two people made an offer to buy the house. She sold the house, paid off the loan and bought a smaller house. My mother taught me about faith, prayer and fasting in times of trouble.

15. Forgiveness

Forgiving my father was a long process for me. There were many unresolved issues with him. Many years later, my younger brother shared with me that when my father was alive, he told him he should take care of his older brother. My younger brother has more education than my older brother. My father may have thought that his youngest son could help his older son. That made me cry. I always thought that my father hated my brother and I grieved over it. This helped me to see good in my father. He still cared for his oldest son.

I still carried resentment toward my father because of the note he left when he died. Twenty seven years after my father's death I had a spiritual experience I will never forget. God helped me to feel my father's deep pain caused by the spirit of torment and despair which led him to commit suicide. I was flooded with tears when I felt my father's pain.

After this experience, I realized my father was the victim of the spirit of torment and despair. I also suffered from torment and despair when my sister died. I finally understood what my father had gone through. He didn't know how to fight the devil's lies that life was not worthwhile. I was healed from pain and torment by God, but my father didn't know how to be healed. This new insight gave me compassion for my father. I was able to forgive my father and let go of my resentment. I am grateful that God helped me to understand my father's pain.

Another time, God gave me a dream where my father looked so happy and told me he liked the food I prepared for him. He even said I was his favorite child. He actually favored my younger sister after I started confronting my father's abusive behavior, so I couldn't understand why he said it. I saw his gentle, kind smile and I felt his love. There were times I felt my father's love when I was little. I used to be his favorite child and he cared for me. In my dream, my father gave me confirmation that he deeply cared for me.

This dream brought so much healing to my heart. I really wanted my father's love. I still feel bad that I wasn't able to reconcile with my father while he was alive, but I am glad that God helped me to see it in my dream. My father had forgiven me. I have forgiven him for all pain he caused, all the tears I shed because of his abusive behaviors. I have forgiven him for taking his life. I hope I will be able to tell him someday that I love him and how much I cared for him when I see him in heaven.

Reflections on Parenting

2. Blessings

1. Moving

About a year after my father's death, my mother was living in a new house. God told her to move. She thought she didn't have any reason to move. After all she lived in that town for more than 20 years and all her friends were there. She also knew that if she sold that house, that would be the last time she would own a home. She cried for many days. Then one day God spoke to her, "Are you that sad that you have to sell the house? I even gave you my own son."

She said, "I am sorry, I will obey you." She sold the house and moved to Seoul. That move turned out to be for my younger brother who was traumatized and suffered so much after our father passed away. God was trying to help my younger brother. Many things were against him. There was no peace at home when our father was alive. He was the one who found our father dead in the bedroom. My brother didn't know how to process grief and loss. When our father was alive my brother had good grades. After our father died, my brother's grades started falling, he had health problems, and struggled.

My brother wanted to be a minister when he was in junior high. My father favored his three daughters, but my brother wanted his love and approval. He thought he could get it when he became a minister. He wanted our father to be proud of him. He told me his dream of becoming a minister died when our father died. How sad! My father not only killed himself, but his son's dream as well. I was glad that my mother decided to move because it helped my brother.

My husband, Keith, was an American. We came to the United States in 1979. We started attending Multnomah Bible

College in Portland, Oregon. After I obtained my citizenship, I invited my mother, my younger brother and sister to America.

2. Gifts

My mother was blessed with the gift of healing. When she prayed for sick people, many were healed. Praying for the sick became her ministry wherever she went. One of my mother's friend's unbelieving husband was suffering from back pain for seven years. My mother prayed for him and he was healed. Thereafter, he started attending church and became a Christian.

One day she went to a church and someone told her about a young woman who was losing her sight. When my mom prayed for her, her eye sight was restored. My mother also led many people to Christ, by inviting them to come to church.

3. Healing

When my mother turned 70 years old, which was 21 years after my father's death, she shared with me how much she suffered from guilt after my father committed suicide. She thought she could have prevented my father's death, but she wasn't able to. For many years, she asked God, "Why? Why did you take him? Why didn't you take me?" It wasn't her fault, but many families who have experienced suicide go through this guilt. My mother was no exception.

She said, "After your father passed away, I grieved a lot. I made many mistakes. I didn't think God could forgive me because I was a terrible sinner. I believed Jesus died for my sins but I didn't think God could forgive me. I cried many times and prayed a lot. I tried to go through the whole Bible every year. And then one day while I was reading the Bible, I felt God was speaking to me through *Isaiah 43:25: 'I, even I, am he who blots out your transgressions, for my own sake, and remembers your sins no more.'* He forgave me not because of me or anything else, but He forgave me for His own sake. It is comforting to know that He wouldn't remember my sins any more. I cried with joy. God convinced me of His love and forgiveness through that Scripture. I was so happy, I couldn't put the Bible down. I held the Bible in my arms as I slept every night for about three months."

I asked, "When did that happen?"

She said, "About five years ago. Then one day, the Lord spoke to me that I was not responsible for my husband's death. After that I haven't suffered from guilt any more."

My mother suffered from guilt for 16 years. I couldn't believe it. I was thankful that God brought healing into her heart. I don't suffer from guilt and shame because I understood that it was my father who made the wrong decision.

4. Grateful

After I made a decision to go into the ministry, I spent more time with my mother while I was attending Iliff School of Theology. I was commuting 430 miles from Buffalo, Wyoming to Denver, Colorado. I did that for three years. During the week days, I stayed at my mother's apartment.

She didn't have an extra bedroom and she insisted that I sleep in her bedroom and she sleep on the couch in the living room. She wanted me to be comfortable and study at her home. She always made me feel special.

The first semester at school, my mother gave me $1000 to help with my tuition. That brought me to tears. I knew that was a lot of money for her. While attending school, I wasn't able to help her with any expenses, but she told me that she was happy to help me with my education. After I graduated from the seminary, my mother moved to Los Angeles to be with my younger brother.

5. Giving

My mother had the gift of fundraising. Many times she motivated others to donate to churches. One time she visited the town where she attended church as a child in Korea. The wall in the sanctuary needed repair. The church was very small and didn't have enough money to fix it. Soon after she came to the States, she raised the money and sent it to the church to repair the wall.

I have a cousin who became a pastor and needed a pulpit and other furniture. My mother again raised the funds and sent him the money for the pulpit and other furniture for his church.

During the time I was attending the seminary, my mother sent $500 to a Korean pastor who sends out DVDs and audio tapes to people all over the world. My mother said, "God is asking me to send this money to the pastor in Korea. The Lord will provide what you need."

I was struggling with finances at the time. She must have felt bad that she wasn't helping me by giving to others. I understood that she should obey the Lord. God provided me with all the funds I needed for school.

6. Encourager

My mother is always encouraging me, especially in my ministry. Whenever I visit or speak with her on the phone, she continuously tells me how proud she is of me. I am amazed at how much my mother helps me to have confidence in myself. All of the credit goes to my Lord Jesus because without His guidance, there is no way I would be in ministry. However, my mother's words tell me that she is happy with what I am doing and that makes me very happy.

7. The Dark Valley

My mother had problems with back pain and weak knees, but she never complained. She was always positive and thankful. In 2010, at 82 years old, she had a stroke and lost her speech. The doctor told my sister and brother to wait six months to find out if she would speak again.

I immediately wanted to fly out to Los Angeles to see her. My brother and sister, who lived close to her told me they were helping her while she was in the hospital. They told me to come out when she was discharged since that is when she would need a lot of help, so I waited.

I was not sure how much time she had left with us. I was in tears while I was praying for her. At the same time, I knew that when God calls her, I should accept it and be thankful. During those days, I was reciting the following Scripture and asking God to help her. *"But those who hope in the LORD will renew their strength. They will soar on wings like eagles; they will run and not grow weary, they will walk and not be faint."* (Isaiah 40: 31) My mother never had to depend on her children for anything until she had a stroke. Her mind was sharp and she prayed for us everyday. When I was praying for her, for the first time, I felt she needed our help to remind her of the power of God's Word.

8. A Miracle

Four days after my mother was hospitalized, I called my brother on Saturday night. I asked him what he was going to do on Sunday morning. He told me he was going to take mother, in her wheelchair, to the worship service in the hospital. I told him she couldn't understand English, so he should lead the worship for her. When my mother prayed for the sick people, she used to recite *Mark 16:17-18*. It says, *"And these signs will accompany those who believe: In my name they will drive out demons; they will speak in new tongues; they will pick up snakes with their hands; and when they drink deadly poison, it will not hurt them at all; they will place their hands on sick people, and they will get well."*

I told my brother that our mother needed to be

reminded of *Mark 16:17-18,* so that she can gain spiritual strength. That night I heard my mother talking in a clear voice in my mind. The Holy Spirit gave me hope that God was going to help her recover.

The next morning, my brother followed my suggestion. My mother asked him to sing a hymn, "Sing Them Over Again to Me." Then she started singing with him and was able to speak. That was a miracle from the Lord! That night my sister called me to tell me that our mother could speak and was recovering very fast. I thanked God for His grace in allowing our mother to be able to speak and have a little more time with us.

9. Recovery

When my mother was discharged, my brother and I brought her home. I made the arrangements for someone to take care of her and do her household chores. I was thankful that my brother was able to move into my mother's apartment to take care of her.

I then asked everyone who was taking care of my mother to read *Luke 4:18-19,* so she could gain her strength and to encourage her. It says, *"The Spirit of the Lord is on me, because he has anointed me to preach good news to the poor. He has sent me to proclaim freedom for the prisoners and recovery of sight for the blind, to release the oppressed, to proclaim the year of the Lord's favor."*

My mother had experienced some loss of memory but she started to recover. Her doctor was surprised that she was recovering so fast. I knew God and her faith were helping her.

10. A Heavenly Song

About four months later, I visited my mother. This time she didn't need others to remind her of the Scriptures. In the early morning, she woke up my brother and myself and led worship. I was so encouraged. She told me that before she had a stroke, she used to spend one hour in the morning and one hour at night worshipping God. She sang hymns for thirty minutes then she read the Bible and prayed. Since she was recovering from her stroke, she was getting back to her regular schedule.

She taught me what was important. Worshipping God is what we are supposed to do while we live on earth. Most of her time is spent reading the Bible, praying and listening to the sermons on television. No wonder she recovered fast. She was relying on the Lord. As soon as my mother was able to get up and function, she started attending church using a walker.

Many years back, when I backslid, I was sad and didn't have joy in my heart. I called my mother, she said, "When I felt sad, I would start singing hymns until I felt better." That made sense. Praising God brings us joy, since we are doing what God wants us to do. But why didn't I know that? I had many years of Bible college training, but I didn't know the importance of praising God through singing hymns until I made the decision to go into the ministry. She was already practicing it in her daily life.

God blessed my mother with spiritual experiences. My mother told me that in the early part of 2010, she heard a beautiful choir singing in the morning. It was one of her favorite hymns, "Far Away in the Depths of My Spirit." At first, she thought someone was singing outside, she rushed out to the hallway, but didn't hear anything. She went outside the building, but there was no one singing. When she went back to her room, she heard the song again. She was so filled with joy. She finally realized that she was listening to a heavenly choir.

11. A Mentor
My younger brother was called to the ministry. He is

a talented singer and a powerful preacher. My mother has been encouraging him to use his gifts to serve the Lord. At one point in his life, my brother struggled and backslid. My mother never gave up hope that someday he would use his gifts and serve the Lord. When I was visiting her, she kept saying that my brother should attend the seminary to finish his Master of Divinity. Korean people value education, and she was telling him that if the lack of education is a hindrance in serving God, then he should finish his degree.

I was skeptical. I didn't think my brother would listen to her. By the next time I visited her, he was attending the seminary. I was amazed by my mother's persuasion. My brother is much happier now.

12. Obedience

While she was recovering from her stroke, my mother was on another mission. This time, she saved $3,000 to help our older brother who would be coming to the United States. He didn't have much money, so she saved to help him. Then the Lord asked her to give everything she had saved for her son to the mission fund.

At this time my brother was attending the seminary, he could have used financial help, but my mother was obeying the Lord by donating all of the money to a seminary. I learned through my mother the importance of obeying the Holy Spirit and the joy of giving. She knew obedience is more important than following her ideas or desires.

13. A Dream

God speaks to me through dreams on different occasions about my family. One day I had a dream that I was with my sister and I saw a bus with my father in it. He looked so young, handsome, and his face was glowing. I went over and brought him out of the bus and took him to where my sister was. I told my sister to ask him some questions, so she tried to talk to him. Suddenly, my father turned into a big framed picture of him, lying on the ground. Then said to my sister, "He is dead and that's why he cannot talk."

When I woke up, I felt God was telling me to contact my sister. I called my sister and told her about my dream and said I had some reservations about if my father was saved or not, but through this dream, I was convinced that he was saved. My father believed in God at some time in his life. As we were talking, I learned that my sister was at a crossroad in her spiritual journey. She told me she had decided not to attend church because attending church didn't help her faith.

I told her she needed to continue to attend church. If she didn't, it would affect her faith and her relationship with God. The first thing she would lose is peace and joy. She agreed that she didn't have peace. I told her that some people wait until they have problems in life, then they turn to God in their misery. Why should she do that? She can have peace and get help from the Lord all the time and also keep growing in faith.

Nothing was getting through to her. I finally mentioned that if our mother has strong faith worshipping God one hour in the morning and one hour at night, and still attends church, there must be a reason for it. Our mother is old and frail but as soon as she was able to walk with a walker, she started attending church.

My sister said, "You are right. I can walk and I had better go to church. I need to repent. When I stopped attending church, my family wouldn't attend church either." She understood that if our mother is doing it, it must be a good thing to do. My mother has been a great example of how we can grow in faith and my sister agrees. I am thankful that God changed my sister's heart.

14. Positive

My mother takes everything, even suffering and pain graciously and is always cheerful, thanking God for everything. She teaches me how we can handle pain with God's help. She is positive about everything even when she has to depend on others to cook and clean the house. She never complained about why God didn't heal her completely. She prayed for many people and they got healed. Why does she have to suffer?

The fact is no one lives forever. Our body is a temporary home for our spirits while we live on earth. She accepted her limitations and her focus was not on living forever here on earth, but to live forever with God in heaven. *"He will wipe every tear from their eyes. There will be no more death or mourning or crying or pain, for the old order of things has passed away." (Revelation 21:4)*

She will have a perfect, healthy body when she is with Jesus. That gives her hope and encouragement. Even though I wanted to have our mother here longer, I understood that she was not going to be with us long, but we will be with her in heaven — forever. I joked about how our bodies are like cars. When our car gets old, things start to come apart and repair is needed. Likewise, my mother is getting old and she needs repairs. We laughed and my mother agreed.

15. Generosity

My mother always thinks about what she can give me whenever I visit her. She is so generous and she doesn't focus on what she can receive from others. When my son visited my mother, she gave him $100 for spending money. That meant a lot to my son. She was not doing well physically, but she still thought about him and tried to show him how much she cared about him. The last time I visited her, she was more concerned about me than herself. She used to fix ginseng for me whenever I visited her before she had a stroke, saying that it would be good for me. She told me she felt bad that she wasn't able to cook for me, and gave me a package of dried ginseng to take home and cook for myself.

16. Grace

I am so blessed to have a mother who has a great love for God and a love for her children and others. She is an example of how a mother can make an impact on her children. She helped me to have faith in God and because of that my life has been a blessing. Because my mother helped me to grow in faith, I learned to see things from a broader and eternal perspective. That gives me peace and encouragement.

It is through God's grace that I experienced healing from the hurts and pains caused by my father. I thank God that I still have a mother who brings healing to my heart and impacts my life in positive ways. She could have been a minister, if she had an education. She has been more than a minister to me. All the pastors I know combined could not help me as much as she did. I thank God for her.

Reflections on Parenting

3. Struggles

1. Unprepared

Parenting is a privilege and children are gifts from God. However, many people become parents without any education on how to nurture their children. That is where we were, when my husband and I had our children. My husband and I never read, studied or attended any parenting classes before or after we had children.

We loved our kids and treasured our time with them. We thought we knew how to raise kids, but in reality, we lacked many things like nurturing and helping them to grow spiritually. How could this happen while my husband was a pastor? Well, it happened. However, we tried our best with what we knew. We had our share of good times and also some challenging times because we made some bad choices.

2. Joy

I was glad that my husband had faith and that we attended church as a family. We had many good times and good memories while they were growing up. When our children were younger, I used to read Bible stories and prayed for them before they went to sleep because I knew how important it is to have faith. I taught my children how to read by reading the Children's Bible to them. It had wonderful pictures for them and they loved it. They both learned how to read before they started school and they excelled in school.

Keith was really good to our children when they were little. My husband brought healing into my heart. I saw how a father could be gentle and kind to children. Our children loved him. They were very close to their dad because he did lots of fun things with them. I learned from my husband that it is important to do fun things with children like playing games, going on trips and fishing together.

3. Everyone Make Mistakes

When our children made a mistake, I told them to say, "Mommy, everyone makes mistakes." This reminded us that we needed to be gentle with one another. No one is perfect and I can not expect our children to be perfect. I would respond to my children, "You are right. Everyone makes mistakes." This became a good practice for us. I did not have to be upset with them knowing we all make mistakes in life.

I always believed in their goodness. They were good kids and when they did make mistakes, they were already feeling bad about their actions. There was no reason for me to hurt them more with guilt and shame. I taught them to learn from their mistakes and to move on.

4. The Lesson

While I was growing up, I had a short temper. I wasn't always kind to my siblings. I suffered from the rage I felt when my father was hitting my mother. I didn't have a good role model except my mother's gentleness and kindness. She had a hard life and had been hurt, but she never lost her temper or harmed us in any way. I never heard her raise her voice or say anything bad to us.

One of my friends visited our home and remarked on how my mother treated her children with love and respect. Her mother cussed at her all the time and didn't show any respect to her own children.

If I made any mistakes, my mother was forgiving. Immediately she tried to help me solve the problem, instead of focusing on a punishment. She gained all of her children's respect and love. My mother was respected by many other people as well.

My mother taught me that we don't have to use harsh discipline or hit our children to correct them. I learned the hard way why harsh discipline is not an effective way of teaching children. One day I got very upset with Fletcher who was stubborn and would not listen to me. He was three or four years old. I lost my temper and spanked him. Afterward, I felt very bad that I had lost my temper. He held resentment against me. I told him I was sorry and asked him to forgive me many times, but he refused. I bought him something he wanted that I normally wouldn't have bought. He agreed to forgive me and he let go of the resentment. I never spanked him again after that. Instead I tried to talk to him when he made mistakes. The lesson I learned from this is that being harsh doesn't pay; it creates dissention and ruins relationships.

5. Reward

Our children were very good to each other, and not once did I need to tell them to be kind to each other. I never saw them fighting as they were growing up. When my son was born, our daughter, Nicole, was happy that she had a brother. When he was sad, she would try to make him laugh. She also told him that if anything happens to their mom and dad, she would take care of him. Our children blessed me and taught me a lot about God's goodness.

I wanted to make sure that our daughter and son didn't have to compete for our love or start to compare themselves with each other. I didn't want to create jealousy between our children. Each one has different gifts. School grades only reflect some of our gifts, not all our gifts. I wanted them to be happy with themselves. Both of our children did well in school but if one of our children received a good grade, I rewarded both of them. We celebrated one's achievement as a family. In that way, they could be happy when the other one did well in school.

6. Mistakes

Keith and I knew the importance of knowing the Bible. We knew that if they watched TV a lot, their values would be affected by worldly standards. God has higher values for us. Life will be peaceful and productive when we have God's higher values. So, if they wanted to watch TV or play video games, we made them read the Bible. One hour of Bible reading made time for one hour of TV or video games. My son later told me that he asked God for wisdom after he read the story of Solomon.

Unfortunately, this only lasted until they became teenagers. As I reflect, the practice of reading and watching TV for equal amounts of time was not good enough to instill God's values in our children. I knew that the worldly influences were so much stronger. I tried to limit the time our children spent on TV watching but because Keith loved watching TV, that didn't work. By the time our children were teenagers, my husband and our children sat together and watched TV. Our children no longer read the Bible in order to watch TV. They justified it as family time. I felt bad that I wasn't able to stop them because it would eventually affect them. I just didn't know the impact of watching so much TV, but Keith and I noticed that when our children watched TV for a long time, they would act nasty to us.

I didn't enjoy watching TV shows and I was critical of what they were watching. I couldn't handle watching violence and all the immoral shows that were made by people who didn't have God's values. Many times when I walked into the living room I would be in shock asking my husband, "What are you watching? Are you watching this kind of show with the kids?" Sometimes they would change the channel, but other times they wouldn't and told me to leave them alone. It was three against one.

Watching too much of worldly shows which didn't have God's values affected our family negatively. I learned that it is easy to waste our time, energy and life on something that is not going to help us grow in faith. Worldly entertainment is a distraction in our spiritual journey, and it takes us to a road on which we can forget about God. We were no longer focused on growing in the Lord together.

7. Lukewarm

Keith and I had several conversations about why we wanted them to attend church, but aside from that we didn't make any intentional efforts to help them grow in faith in our daily life. We never had any family devotion and didn't pray together in peaceful times or when we faced challenges. We didn't read the Bible together as a family or had discussions about faith. I believe this is one of the reasons why our family values started to deteriorate and affected our faith negatively.

While my husband was working as a minister, I struggled with my own faith. I was attending church on Sunday morning, but rarely read the Bible. I almost lost my faith and struggled. Even so, I could see how easy it was for my family to be entertained by shows that didn't contribute to spiritual growth and instead were detrimental to our faith and against God's values.

I believe this was one of the reasons why our family struggled a lot when our children became teenagers. Their hearts were not focused on growing in faith because we weren't able to help them to develop a close relationship with the Lord. In fact, I myself didn't have a close relationship with the Lord. Therefore, I didn't know how to help our children.

As parents, we didn't see the big picture of what we did wrong and we didn't see what was coming. I believe our ignorance and lack of concern for our children's spiritual growth contributed to our children's rebellion.

8. Struggles

My husband and I didn't have any problems with our children when they were younger. They were perfect children and we maintained a good relationship with them until they became teenagers. We never expected or imagined that we would have any problems with them.

One day I had a terrible dream that my daughter and my husband were in a muddy river. I was on a bridge with my son. In a panic, I was frantic and shouting loudly to get my husband's attention that our daughter disappeared in the river, but he didn't seem to realize it. When I woke up from my dream, I was flooded with fear. At the time my daughter started resisting going to church.

I cried for many days and feared for my daughter. I was concerned about her salvation. I was so desperate and I was pleading with God to help her. I wept for others, but I wept for her more than anyone else. The Lord helped me in times of trouble. He told me He was greater than my problems and asked me to give my daughter to Him. God started teaching me to rely on Him and not worry.

There were many things that were against our children's spiritual growth. If Keith had not been a pastor, we would have attended a church that had a strong youth program for our children. All of the congregations he served were in small towns where there were very few young people, so they weren't able to connect with other young kids who had faith and were growing in the Lord.

Another problem we had was when our children reached their teenage years, they didn't want to attend church anymore when they started having problems with their dad. They didn't want to go to church where their father preached. We tried hard to make them attend church but they resisted. We got tired of fighting.

Finally, we told them to find a church they wanted to attend. They said they were going to church but they didn't always follow what we asked of them. I understood that they needed to seek their own faith and relationship with the Lord, but I wished we were able to help them to be more involved with the church and with God.

9. A Mentor

In the midst of all the troubles of raising our kids, I felt so helpless. Then the Lord started guiding me to help them in ways I never expected.

In 2000, my first year of school, Nicole was dating a man. I had a dream that she was dating another man. After I woke up, God told me that Nicole needed a mentor, because difficult times were coming. I never even thought about finding a mentor for her until that day. God told me I needed to ask Michelle Hannan to be her mentor. She was a member of Buffalo United Methodist Church (UMC), where my husband was the pastor.

That day, I drove to Denver to attend school. That evening I called Michelle and asked her if she would be a mentor to Nicole. She told me that when our church was talking about mentoring young people, she had thought about Nicole and that she would be glad to be Nicole's mentor.

That was one of the best things to happen to my daughter. All throughout her high school years, every Wednesday night, Michelle picked Nicole up, took her home, where she fixed meals for her and spent time with her. Not long after that Nicole and her boyfriend broke up. She went through a rough time. Michelle was there for Nicole and encouraged her.

During Nicole's teenage years, she had a tough time with her dad because of Keith's temper. After our family moved to Colorado, Nicole decided to stay in Buffalo to finish high school. Rev. Sue Debris became the pastor of Buffalo UMC and took care of Nicole and mentored her. Nicole was able to live in the parsonage in the same room when we stayed in Buffalo. That was another blessing. I am forever thankful for these two women who took care of my daughter. Nicole turned out to be a very responsible and caring person as she always had been. I am so proud of her. I have many regrets about how I wasn't able to help her, but I believe having two Christian mentors in her life has helped her immensely.

10. Reflection

Why did we have so many problems at home? There were many reasons and everyone of us contributed to them. After God healed me from backsliding, he called me to the ministry. To my surprise, my husband was not supportive of my decision to go into the ministry. He refused to move to Denver where I could attend seminary. He told me to commute and I was commuting to school for three years and I was gone a lot. We had struggles of our own so we had less time and energy to pay attention to our children's needs. Not only that, our children didn't follow the things we taught them to avoid the troubles in life but they followed the advice of their friends. My husband didn't know how to handle our children and he lost his temper. I couldn't convince him to be gentle and kind to our children. We went through many storms and I thought if we can survive those, we will come out stronger. I thank God that He was helping us with parenting even though we made many mistakes.

11. A Mission Project

God also started helping my son when we were going through a very difficult time. Fletcher had always excelled in school and had faith in God since he was a child. His grades started failing during his teenage years when he started having problems with his dad. Keith was very critical and had a negative attitude toward Fletcher that hurt our son deeply.

By the time I finished my school, my husband finally decided to move to Colorado. Fletcher insisted on staying in Buffalo but he couldn't do that since he was too young to take care of himself. He was a freshman in high school when we moved to Keenesburg, Colorado. After we moved, we went through a storm. Fletcher dropped out of high school. He wanted to go back to Buffalo High School, so I took him to Buffalo. He stayed at his friend's home and attended school, but that didn't work out. He moved back home. We couldn't convince him to finish high school.

I asked him to get a GED and get it over and start college. I took him to a community college and he passed all the tests with high scores. He received his GED when he was 15. But Fletcher told me that he wanted to attend a private high school and get a high school diploma. So, we enrolled him in a private Catholic school. He failed all the classes and dropped out after one semester. Our family went through a tough time. Not being able to help our son was one of the hardest times we had gone through. I cried many days asking God to help Fletcher.

Keith and Fletcher couldn't get along. I felt so helpless. I was in turmoil in those days. There was no peace at home so I got an apartment for Fletcher. He started taking classes at a community college, but was failing all the classes. He didn't have clear goals of what he wanted to do with his life. He lacked motivation.

I was very upset and worried about my son. I constantly prayed and asked God to help him. The Lord said, "He is my mission project." I never thought about seeing my son as a mission project. After all, everyone is God's mission project. I thought if God considers my son as a mission project, then I should see him as a mission project.

Immediately, I was able to let go of my resentment and anger. If the Lord hadn't mentioned anything about it, I would never have thought about sending him into the mission field.

I met with my son and I said to him, "You have four options. First, if you do well in school, then I will support you. Second, if you don't want to attend school, then quit school and go get a job so you can take care of yourself. Third, you spoke about joining the military. If that's what you want, then join the military. Fourth, if you want to go on a mission trip, I will sponsor you."

I also told him I would not support his school since he was failing all the classes, and I would not continue to pay for his apartment. He had to come home or make a decision to do something else. He decided to go on a mission trip. Within a week, when I met a youth pastor at Broomfield United Methodist Church, he told me he was going on a mission trip to Mexico for two years. I told him Fletcher was interested in going on a mission trip and asked if he could go with him. He said yes, so my son went with him.

12. Hannah's Prayer

After my son left for Mexico, God asked me to pray like Hannah who was Samuel's mother who dedicated her son to the Lord before he was even conceived.

"In bitterness of soul Hannah wept much and prayed to the LORD. And she made a vow, saying, 'O LORD Almighty, if you will only look upon your servant's misery and remember me, and not forget your servant but give her a son, then I will give him to the LORD for all the days of his life, and no razor will ever be used on his head.'"(1 Samuel 1:10-11)

God answered Hannah's prayer and she had a son, Samuel. After he was weaned, Hannah took him to the temple where a priest named Eli served the Lord. Samuel was a young boy when he heard God's voice. He served the

Lord for the rest of his life as a faithful servant.

At first, I couldn't understand why God asked me to pray like Hannah. I knew that my son is not mine, but is the Lord's. I prayed as the Lord asked me to pray: "Lord Jesus, I give my son to your work for the rest of his life." Since then I prayed this prayer whenever I was concerned about my son. It gave me comfort.

A month later, my son called me from Mexico and asked me if I could make arrangements for him to go on a mission trip to Korea. He told me he didn't want to come home because he didn't want to be with his dad. If God didn't ask me to pray for my son as He did, I would have responded, "You told me you will be gone only two months and when you come back, you will go back to school. Why do you need to go on a mission trip again? It would cost a lot if you go to Korea. Just come back and go back to school."

God prepared my heart by asking me to pray like Hannah. I knew it was good that my son wanted to go to Korea. At first, I thought about sending him to my home town, where I knew a pastor who had a 600 member congregation including an English worship service and it had an American associate pastor.

Then a thought crossed my mind, and I believe it was God speaking to me. "Why not send him to the largest church in the world?" I made arrangements with the Full Gospel Church in Korea, which was the largest church in the world, about 760,000 members. My son stayed in Korea for six months. One of the jobs he had was typing Pastor Yong Ki Joe's sermons. What a blessing! My son had the chance to type wonderful sermons and he was proud of what he was doing. When he returned home, I was amazed by his growth and maturity.

First, my son made an effort to repair the relationship with his dad. My husband couldn't do it, but my son spent time with his dad and took the initiative to restore their relationship. I couldn't believe what I was seeing. One of the reasons why he wanted to go to Korea on a mission trip was because he didn't want to be with his dad. My son's attitude toward his dad was indifferent. He didn't attend his dad's church for years. We gave up on that, but he decided to attend a youth retreat where his dad was one of the retreat leaders. This made my husband and I very happy.

Second, my son became motivated to go back to school. He first applied to Colorado University but his grades from community college were so poor that they told him to apply if he can prove that he can handle the classes. He applied Metro College and was accepted. He moved out of the house, found a part time job and attended school. I supported his school and he passed all the classes with good grades. A year later, he was accepted to Colorado University in Denver. He has been excelling in all classes and receiving scholarships. I didn't have to tell him to do well in school; he was already motivated to do so. That was a miracle. I thank God for helping my son.

13. Healing

After finishing high school, my daughter got married and she is very happy. Her mother-in-law and father-in-law are very gentle and nurturing people. They treat my daughter as if she was one of their own. My daughter is again surrounded with loving and caring people and I thank God for them.

When Nicole had her first child, it brought healing into our family. We had get-togethers and spent time with our granddaughter. Keith loved our grandchildren and he was good to them. I was glad that my daughter's relationship with her dad was better after she got married.

God knew my concern about my daughter's salvation for a long time. One day while I was listening to a song, "Be Not Afraid," suddenly the Lord spoke to me that my daughter was saved. I was flooded with tears of gratefulness. Since then, I don't worry about my daughter's salvation. I just thank God for helping me realize that my daughter is saved. She gave her life to the Lord when she was little and I know God is taking care of her.

14. Forgiveness

On July 9, 2008, my husband died in a tragic car accident. Losing Keith so suddenly was very difficult for all of us, but I was thankful that he had a good relationship with Fletcher before he passed away. Fletcher suggested that we should have lunch once a week and spend time together right after my husband's death. We shared a lot of unresolved things together and continuously processed grief and pain caused by Keith's death. It also strengthened our relationship. As I got to know more about my son, the more he impressed me by his maturity.

I went through a very tough time and was immobilized with grief and pain, but God brought healing into my heart. I was able to let him go and function again. I shared with my children that God brought healing to my heart so they don't have to worry about me. I couldn't help them when I was going through my grieving process but now I can focus on their healing. They both loved their dad and this sudden loss was very difficult for them.

I know there were still some unresolved issues between my husband and my son. It would have been better if Keith and Fletcher were able to have more conversations with each other to resolve everything, but time was not in their favor. My son once asked me, "Mom, do you think I have forgiven my dad?" I said, "Did you tell God that you forgive your dad in tears?" He said, "No, I haven't done that." I replied, "Then, you haven't forgiven him."

I told him he needs to forgive his father or it will affect his relationship with others. He said he understood what I meant and he knew that forgiving his dad would take some time. As time went on, I followed up with my son about forgiving his dad and he responded that he had forgiven his dad. This made me very happy.

The lesson I wanted to teach my son about forgiveness was that until we forgive we cannot move on with life. We are immobilized by pain and grief. I thanked Fletcher many times for reaching out to his dad before he passed away. My husband loved our children deeply, but didn't know how to build a good relationship with them during their adolescent years. I am glad to see that God helped my children to reach out to their dad before he passed away.

15. Grace

I have learned that God cares about every aspect of my life, including my parenting. From time to time, He has helped me to help my children by allowing me to understand what they were going through. God gave me a vision of my son. I saw my son all curled up in the palms of God's big hands. All over my son's body were these cracks, like a broken vase glued back together.

I cried after having this vision. It gave me compassion and a better understanding for my son. I pray that God will bring healing to my children. Many times God has assured me that He is leading and helping my children. That brings me comfort. The Lord teaches me to let go of my worry and fear which can be distractions in my relationship with the Lord and in my ministry. I am thankful for that.

16. Kindness

I try to maintain good relationships with my children. I do not want us to have any unresolved issues between us. Every chance I get, I try to ask my children to forgive me for not being available when they needed me. I went to school for personal reasons, but my children will not understand that. I will continue to do this until they can completely let go of their hurts and resentment caused during my absence in their lives.

My daughter has four children and she is a very patient and caring mother. I am blessed to be around her. She always has a calm presence and she takes care of her children with love and respect. I told my daughter many times how proud I am of her parenting skills and what a wonderful daughter she is to me. I am thankful for my children.

My son has started to open up to my ideas and suggestions. He would say, "Mom, tell me what you have learned from life so I don't have to live many years trying to figure it out." I explained to him the importance of loving God, reading the Bible, listening to God, and serving others. I told him if he wants happiness, helping others is the key because selfish people are miserable people. They only focus on what they can get and what they didn't get; but, when they think about what they can give to make other people happy, they will be filled with joy and happiness. Recently, my son told me that I am his role model. That made me very happy.

17. Surrender

I love my children but I know my first love and priority is loving God, then I can love my children. All I have are temporary gifts, including my children, and that helps me to rely on God more than anyone or anything. This gives me peace. If I put my children first, I would be living in fear and worry. I have no control over their decisions or how they want to live because they are adults. I gave my children to the Lord. I cannot always be with them but God can and He will. I know if they have faith, they will be able to handle problems and struggles with God's wisdom. I am praying that God will bless them in all areas of life.

The Ultimate Parenting Guide

Reflections on Parenting

4. Regrets

The following story was published in the Chaplain's column in Adams County Detention Facility inmates' newsletter, "Passing Times." This article is written to help parents by explaining how God helped me to see the big picture of my weaknesses in parenting and what was my regrets and how I repented.

"The Last Penny"

When I was in Korea, I met a missionary who told me that somehow Korean people never get out of the repentant mode. He said, "Once you have repented, you are saved and you don't need to repent again." I told him that he misunderstood the biblical understanding of repentance. There are two aspects of repentance, I told him.

First, repentance happens when we recognize that we are sinners in need of God's forgiveness that comes through Jesus, who died on the cross for our sins. We repent also when we realize that God can save us, not by our good works, but by believing in Jesus through faith and the great mercy of God.

Second, we need to repent daily, moment by moment, when we fall into sin to be purified and to be forgiven, so we can live a life that will please God. Being saved doesn't mean that you automatically become a saint, or become an angel overnight or are released from all temptations and sinful desires. You still have to learn God's values and standards by studying the Bible and resisting temptation and sin. My understanding of repentance is the same even today.

Paul wrote, *"Therefore, I urge you, brothers, in view of God's mercy, to offer your bodies as living sacrifices, holy and pleasing to God — this is your spiritual act of worship. Do not conform any longer to the pattern of this world, but be transformed by the renewing of your mind. Then you will be able to test and approve what God's will is — his good, pleasing and perfect will."* (Romans 12:1-2)

In order to be transformed, we need to keep making changes in our attitudes and behaviors. This process is a repenting process. Some call it sanctifying grace.

Many of us have developed many destructive attitudes and behaviors. We have a mental file cabinet named, "un-repented sins" and we are not even aware that we have it. To be transformed in our hearts and lives, we need to go through it and get rid of anything that needs to be repented for to forgive and be forgiven.

John said, *"If we claim we have not sinned, we make him out to be a liar and his word has no place in our lives."* (1 John 1:10) Living in sin invites the devil to control our lives instead of being led by the Holy Spirit. Confessing our sins is very important. When we repent, God can help us. Also, 1 John 1:9 says, *"If we confess our sins, he is faithful and just and will forgive us our sins and purify us from all unrighteousness."*

If there is anything that you feel is not right, it is about time to ask the Lord for help. You can pray, "Lord, is there any sin for which I need to repent? Is there anyone that I hurt and have not repented? Is there anything that you see in me that needs to be changed? Is there any sin I committed with my mouth? Please help me to recognize it so I can make changes and be transformed."

In December 2009, I took the word "repentance" very seriously. In 2010, as a new year's resolution, I decided to ask the Lord to point out areas that I need to repent. In the past, I repented from time to time when God pointed out what I did wrong, or when my conscience started bothering me, or when others pointed out what I did wrong. I never asked God to help me to repent or make repentance my highest priority. I can tell you I am glad that I asked God for help. He has been revealing things that I didn't even think about before.

There are four reasons why I decided to focus on repenting: First, even though we may profess that we are Christians, many of our values can be affected by worldly values instead of God's values. Thus, we justify our sin. After David committed adultery and murder, he didn't repent. God sent the prophet Nathan to confront David's sin and he repented. *(2 Samuel 12:13)*

Second, our memory is limited. Sometimes without God's help, we really cannot remember or recognize our sin. However, God remembers it and He wants us to repent.

Third, many times we cannot see the big picture God sees. We are rebellious and develop a wrong perception and/or attitude toward something or someone and don't even realize it. This comes from our sinful nature.

Fourth, Jesus told us to repent. *"From that time Jesus began to preach, and to say, repent: for the kingdom of heaven is at hand."* (Matthew 4:17) He also said, *"I tell you the truth, you will not get out until you have paid the last penny."* (Matthew 5:23) Jesus said he will not let us get away with what we owe. So, think about what you owe to God, yourself, your family, and others and ask God to help you repent.

Since I started praying, to my surprise (although I shouldn't have been surprised), God started showing me what I needed to repent one by one. I am still working on that and will until I die. I know the sooner I recognize my sin and repent, the sooner I will be able to grow. God was helping me to see things that I wasn't able to see before. As I started seeing the big picture, I saw many things I needed to change. I started making changes in my priorities and started working on areas which I had neglected.

One area for which I repented was how I raised my children. For a while, I kept asking God to help them to grow in faith and their love for the Lord and others. Then, God started revealing to me, why my children are the way they are. While they were growing up, I was a lukewarm Christian. I didn't have love for the Lord, nor the desire to serve the Lord. I fell into the sin of loving worldly possessions more than God. He was not my first priority in life, but security and building up material things were. I struggled a lot when God called me to ministry because I loved the world more than Him.

That doesn't mean that I totally neglected my children. My husband was a pastor and our children grew up in the church. We took them to church and tried to tell them of God's values, until they started their rebellious stage. They had no idea what it meant to love the Lord. I wasn't able to teach them because I didn't have those values either. So, I repented in tears.

Our children turned out to be good. I have a wonderful relationship with them, and I am thankful for it. But, I still want them to learn to love the Lord and serve the Lord more fully than they have. I cannot change the past, so what do I need to do to help them?

I am encouraged by what Jesus had said to a man who brought a sick son to him for healing. *"He said, 'It has often thrown him into fire or water to kill him. But if you can do anything, take pity on us and help us.' 'If you can?' said Jesus. 'Everything is possible for him who believes.' Immediately the boy's father exclaimed, 'I do believe; help me overcome my unbelief!'"* Mark *(9:22-24)* Jesus heals the boy and the father's request was granted. Also, Jesus gives direction to parents on what to do. On the way to the cross, Jesus said, *"Daughters of Jerusalem, do not weep for me; weep for yourselves and for your children." (Luke 23:28)*

Jesus gives us clear direction on what concerned

parents should do: Have faith in God, pray and weep for your children. Even if you have faith and pray and are a good example, some children might not follow your example because of a rebellious heart. So, what do you do in that case? As a parent, you should not give up in any case, keep praying for them. God will send someone else to help them grow in faith. If you feel you have not been a good example, it's time to repent and ask God to help you. Start now to be a good influence. It's not too late for anyone to change.

As I thought about how we can help our children, besides working on our faith and praying for them, I have learned that many parents have attitudes, words, and actions that show disrespect for their children.

Don't speak words that do not have a positive impact. As parents, when we speak defeating words to our children, they pick up on it and act on it. I have seen the detrimental effects of it from my father who hated my brother. He called him many bad names and, unfortunately, it all came true. How sad! We need to think before we speak, especially when we speak to our children. *"The tongue has the power of life and death, and those who love it will eat its fruit."* (Proverbs 18:21)

There is so much power in spoken words. Parents, you have so much power to help your children succeed. Even while incarcerated, they desperately need your love and confirmation. You are the only parents they will ever have in their lifetime.

If you have not been treating your children with love and respect, it is time to repent and change your ways. Some might have to ask for forgiveness for bad attitudes and words that have hurt their children. You might have to ask for forgiveness from your children for not being available.

I had to ask my children to forgive me for the times I was not there when they needed me. In addition, you have to show them how much you love them by taking care of yourself and taking care of their needs. You can be a positive influence to your children. Even adult children need your continued emotional and spiritual support. They have a need to feel that you care about them. It all depends on what you say and what you do.

Lastly, develop a habit of proclaiming victory in Christ. The words you proclaim will make a difference. With God's help, you will see miracles. I decided to proclaim victory for my children. "I proclaim victory in Christ, that my children will be blessed spiritually, mentally, emotionally, physically, financially, and with relationships so they will be surrounded with godly people. I proclaim that my children will be able to love the Lord and love themselves and others for the glory of God. I proclaim victory, that they will be a blessing to their families and themselves. I proclaim victory that they will be able to use their gifts to serve God and help others."

Again, I ask you to pray the victory prayer for yourself. "I claim victory in Christ, that I will be a blessing to everyone, especially to my children. I claim victory, that my children will be blessed by my transformation in Christ. I claim victory that God is going to help my children."

You can proclaim and say, "There will be no defeating words or curse words coming out of my mouth anymore, but words of blessings to everyone, especially my children and my family. Lord, I bless you. I bless my mouth. I bless my children, my family, and my friends. Let me be a blessing to everyone."

Keep proclaiming victory in Christ and you will see victory. Your words have much more power than you think and God has given you the gift of word to bless Him and bless others, especially your children and family. Pay the last penny you owe, especially to your children, by blessing them through your faith, words, actions and prayer.

Chapter 2

The Lessons

1. "THE LESSONS" by Donna Tabor

I was six months old when my mom was taken. I was there when it happened. My uncle killed my mother with a brick and there was blood everywhere. They tried to save her life but it was too late. My grandparents tried to raise us. Out of nine of us, I am the youngest. When I was one year old, I was sent to an orphanage called the Southern Christian Home. All of my siblings were there except my oldest brother. He stayed with my grandparents.

I was molested when I was seven years old but no one believed me. I tried to tell, but no one would listen to me. When the people that raised me stopped working at the orphanage, I was devastated. I was 13 years old when that happened and I started to hate the world. I started getting high to kill the pain in my heart. I didn't want to think about what I had to do. I started using my body for drugs. I would sell my body and I went to jail when I was 15 years old. I thought that was love. I knew about Jesus and God but I really didn't know much about faith or having a relationship with God.

The lesson that I had to learn was that I had to let go and let God work in my life. Jesus started talking to me. But I was saying, "Who are you? How can I trust you? I have never trusted in you." He spoke to my heart. "I am not like any other man. I love you, Donna. I made you. I formed you in your mother's womb. I died for you." At that moment, I was filled with the Holy Spirit and fire. I was 22 years old and praying in tongues. Jesus touched my heart.

I do thank God for my life. I know He has a plan for

me. The Scripture says, "'For I know the plans I have for you,' declares the LORD, 'plans to prosper you and not to harm you, plans to give you hope and a future.'" (Jeremiah 29:11)

How was I able to forgive my uncle that killed my mother? Again, the Holy Spirit started speaking to me, "How can I forgive you if you cannot forgive?" I had to let go and let God take control. My brother was in prison at the time. I went to see him and my uncle was at the same prison my brother was at. We sat at the table to see each other. My uncle was sitting at the table also and that's when the Lord spoke to me, "Now is the time." I started talking to him. He could not say anything. All he could do was look. It was time for the visiting to be over. We could take pictures before we left.

When it was time to say our good-byes, I walked over to my uncle and gave him a hug good-bye. At that moment in my heart I said to myself and God, "Jesus, I forgave him." I felt free in my heart. It has been very hard growing up knowing I would not see or talk to my mother. But the Holy Spirit, my comforter, started talking to my heart. I heard the Lord Jesus speak to me. He said, "You will see her." I was doing drugs to kill the pain. I do find peace with Jesus. He is everything I need and more. Jesus is my Mother and my Father and my friend. Jesus, He is all and He is number one. He is that great. One of my favorite verses in the Bible is Psalm 91:11: "For he will command his angels concerning you to guard you in all your ways." "A song of ascents. I lift up my eyes to the hills — where does my help come from?" (Psalm 121:1)

My regret about being a parent was, here I am having children when I was 18 years old. I have three wonderful children. I put two of them up for adoption when they were four and five years old. I had to give them to Jesus. I could not do it any more. I got tired of dragging them here and there. They saw me being abused. It has been a long journey.

I know God can do anything. 14 years later I saw them for the first time, and oh what a joy. God can do miracles. He does miracles everyday if you only believe. I kept believing I would see them someday. I kept having faith. My 21 year old daughter has a son. I am a proud grandmother. My son is doing well. We still have to work on some things. In time Jesus will work it all out. I do have a nine year old and she does not know me. My relatives have raised her. I put my children in the Lord's hands and I know they are safe. *"I can do everything through him who gives me strength."* *(Philippians 4:13)* *"But seek first his kingdom and his righteousness, and all these things will be given to you as well."* *(Matthew 6:33)*

2. "I FORGIVE HIM" by Alejandro Garcia

I grew up in the poorest place of all the neighborhoods in Las Vegas, Nevada. My three brothers, little sister, and myself. Mom and Dad were still together and sort of happy I guess. I went to school and came home to the loving family that we had. Nothing seemed wrong with my parents, that is what my brothers and I thought.

It all started when my dad lost interest in my mom. They were fighting constantly, verbally and physically. It was pretty traumatizing for all of us children. When they fought, my dad usually would take control, beat my mom and make her cry in front of us. It was something that happened a lot so we got used to the violence. My dad got caught by a neighbor and got taken away by the police. I thought in my head that my dad did nothing bad and was being taken away by bad cops.

What I did not realize is that my mom was suffering from this abuse, physically and mentally. It happened all the way until I was 13 to 14 years old. My mom couldn't do this anymore for the sake of her children and herself. She called the cops and they tackled him down to the floor and took him away. My mom got that problem taken care of and moved on. She was the mother and father in the relationship with her kids from then on. She was my hero and my role model. She took care of bills, and worked hard just to keep her kids alive while my dad was being ignorant and went off with another woman rather than taking care of his kids.

My dad neglected us for most of our lives. Once we were all grown, he realized that he needed to start participating in his sons and daughters lives. All my brothers blew him off and wanted nothing to do with my dad except me. I still take his advice as father to son. I told him that I will always love him because he brought me into this life even though he hasn't been there for me. I gave him a hug and told him, "I love you dad and I forgive you. I don't hold a grudge against you and we all make mistakes." I forgave my father, God told me to forgive and not carry a grudge against him. In order for me to be forgiven, I have to forgive first. And I want my kids to have a grandpa to go to. The Scripture says, *"If it is possible, as far as it depends on you, live at peace with everyone." (Romans 12:18)*

3. "HE HEALED MY HEART" by Jeanette Aragon

I am 30 years old and a mother of three beautiful children. I have been in and out of jail for the last seven years. I lost my mother on December 30, 2003. She passed away with cirosis of the liver. Sad to say I turned to alcohol. I didn't know how to cope with the pain so I numbed myself by drowning my sorrow.

I hated my mom for being so selfish and drinking herself to death. I hurt more because I had many unanswered questions to why she didn't raise my brother and I. Growing up all I ever wanted was to be loved by my mother. I lived my life trying to make her happy, trying to earn her love and at the same time I held a grudge because she was never there. My aunt and uncle raised my brother and I. My mom's older sister whom I respect, love and honor for loving me, but it was not the same. I wanted my mother's love.

I have memories of my mom when she would come and see me, make broken promises and reek of alcohol and Aquanet hairspray. She would lay on my bed and tell me that we would be a family again someday, then she would leave. I wouldn't see her again for months.

I cried myself to sleep with the scent of her smell on my pillow. I was young like eight or nine but I knew that pain in my heart was from a broken heart.

I have forgiven my mother for my hurt, hate and grudges which I carried to her death bed. The unanswered questions I had for her have been answered by myself because I have followed her same footsteps. I never thought in a million years I would hurt my children the way my mom hurt me. But I sit here, incarcerated at ACDF, and my family is taking care of my kids.

It is like a cycle in my family. My grandmother did it to my mom. My mom did it to me and now I need to break that. I don't want my kids growing up feeling the way I have. I have every opportunity to change. I will do things differently, talk to my kids about what has happened in the past and close that chapter for a new beginning.

My 14 year old is already heading down my path and it hurts my heart. Communication is the one thing I never had from my mother and it is the most important thing I have with my kids. I've learned a lot from my experiences with my mom even though she is not here to teach me. I'm still learning from her. I've also realized that she loved me the whole time. She just didn't know how to express herself. I miss her like crazy but things happen for a reason. I know she is in a better place. She is not hurting anymore and I have learned from our experience how to be a better mother to my children. Thanks to God who has made my faith stronger. He has healed my heart.

4. "FORGIVENESS" by Eli Sandoval

I had a good childhood...at least until my folks got divorced when I was eight years old. Even after they split, the loving bond between both my parents and myself remained and they rarely allowed any tension between each other to be evident to me. I am sure it was very difficult for them to pretend all was well between them and I cannot thank them enough for their efforts.

I believe, deep down, I felt responsible for my parent's break-up. However I was not conscious of that for many years but, looking back, it explains a lot of the poor decisions I have made as well as most of the 'bad' habits I have become accustomed to over the course of my life.

Those 'bad' habits and decisions began with stealing cigarettes and smoking regularly by the age of nine followed by drinking as well shortly after that. The use of marijuana by the time I was ten or eleven lead to weekly doses of LSD that continued, along with the rest, until my dear friend, Sean, never fully recovered from a 'trip' we took one summer evening at the age of 14. Unfortunately he was not the same person ever again. Since middle school, I have had repeated run-ins with the law, all of which have been misdemeanor offenses...until now. I am, currently, an inmate at ACDF awaiting a decision for reinstatement of I.S.P., a community corrections sentence, or a possible prison term. I have peace about the outcome because I have prayed for forgiveness as well as God's will over the future of my life.

I have been very angry with life and the Lord due to the losses of my son at 14 months of age and two of my closest friends. Sean ended up committing suicide shortly after the death of my sweet baby boy and Ty, who lost his life in an alcohol related incident back in July 1997...God rest their souls. It has taken many years for the Lord to teach me that as much forgiveness as we seek for our own sins from him, the least we can do is forgive others for the few times they have wronged us. *"Forgive us our sins, for we also forgive everyone who sins against us."* (Luke 11:4a)

I do not blame my parents for the decisions they have made, nor do I hold them responsible for problems in my own life over the years. Both of them have since been re-married and I am very grateful for their happiness and for the relationships I have with all of them as well as their love and continued support. I've realized that it is myself I needed to forgive, not my parents. Parents need to support their kids all through life, it is so important. One day children will need to take care of their parents as well. However, life is what it is and it is as tough to be a parent as it is to be a kid and we all make mistakes. It is nobody's fault, it is a part of life.

We love them and they love us despite our shortcomings, that's what 'family' is all about. Parents/children... they need our forgiveness as much as we need theirs just as we all need God to forgive us! That is how God teaches us to forgive others as well as ourselves and that matters most. *"Forgive us our debts, as we also have forgiven our debtors."* (Matthew 6:12) Thank you Jesus for His grace, mercy, and forgiveness!

Although the hurts and pains of life are more than tough to get through and it's even tougher to overcome the blame involved, there is a great peace God brings to our lives when we seek His healing and allow Him to renew our spirit while strengthening our hearts and minds. It's not easy to forgive and to let go of all the bitterness and resentment. But with the grace and mercy of the Lord, we are afforded the ability not only to survive desperate and lonely times but to become better witnesses for Christ and what He can and will do for us when the life He gave us seems too much to bear.

5. "HE ANSWERED ME" by Mireya Vizcarra

Today, May 30, 2011, nearly 23 years have passed. At

a very young age, I had the most terrible and painful experience of my life. I suffered physical and mental abuse from a man and soon after I was pregnant by him. That gave me the strength and courage to leave him. I was in a place unknown to me and away from my family. I had been living in California for the last 23 years.

I gave birth to a baby girl. She made me feel proud about myself and was the reason why I should keep moving forward in my life. My mother and sisters came from Mexico to welcome the new member of our family. Their hearts were full of love for my daughter. Two months after she was born, we were on our way to our first vacation in Mexico (my daughter, mother, sister and a cousin). We went on this trip and were very excited. I was driving.

My daughter was next to me and my mother was holding her. While I was passing through a little town between 5:00 a.m. and 6:00 a.m., I had an experience that I had never felt before. I felt like we were in a heavenly place, floating. Everybody was sleeping but my daughter and I. We were looking at each other, directly in the eyes. I never thought that would be my last time seeing her eyes open. She probably wanted to tell me that she would miss me and that she loved me too.

Soon after I fell asleep, what felt like just for a few seconds, all of a sudden I woke up, it was too late. Oh no! What happened next was a horrible experience. I was trying to control the car that was already out of control. I have no idea how many times the car rolled over. When it stopped, the car was on top of me on the highway. People stopped to help us. I was fully conscious and concerned for the baby. I cried, "Please find my baby! Look for her! I am okay."

They were digging a hole so my body would not suffer the pressure of the car. Why me? How? I couldn't believe all this was happening to me. I was in indescribable pain. It was the most horrible experience I've ever had or I could ever imagine going through. Help arrived. My daughter and my mother were the first to be transported to a hospital in a helicopter. My sister, cousin and I were transported to the hospital by ambulance.

My daughter was dead and my mother was in a coma, with only a 20% chance of survival. If she did survive she might be in a vegetative state or mentally ill. I was angry at God and asked, "If you really exist, why is this happening? Why am I alive? Why did I survive? Why am I not dead too? That way I would not be feeling this horrible pain. Why? My daughter was the only reason for me to fight for life. She was taken from my arms." My suffering, grieving and pain wasn't enough. This was my fault. I am guilty. I was the driver. I killed my own daughter.

After three months, my mother responded. She was disabled, suffered enough brain damage, not to be normal ever again. Since then my anger was like a seed in my heart, growing. I didn't realize that the anger was covering my pain and tears. My personality and my character was changed over night. I did not tolerate mistakes or wrong from anyone. I was hiding my grief, pain and anger, only focusing on succeeding in life, working many hours, and exhausting my mind and body.

My mother suffered for more than 18 years after the accident. After she passed away my anger grew. I didn't talk to any of my sisters anymore. Two and a half years passed by. I started reading a Catholic Bible, the Bible started to open my eyes and my heart. I asked God many questions. My understanding of Jesus' love, his life and the suffering was my breaking point.

Today He answered questions that I had been asking Him 23 years ago. Why did I survive? Why was I alive? Why didn't I die in that accident? With a very loud, calm, kind and soft voice, He spoke to me. He had a purpose for me. His will for me in life wasn't done. He definitely wants me to tell others that He loves us, He forgives us and to forgive every single one that hurts us or has done something wrong to us.

After understanding the real reason of Jesus Christ's crucifixion was to forgive all my sins, I was able to forgive myself and others as well. I started to change. That is when I learned to be humble and to have compassion for myself and others. Forgiving was my master key. Using it helped me to open a door that hindered me from a walk to the other side and finding the real me: the person that God wanted me to be, with a heart to use to love Him first and then others. I really love Him. I can't stop it. I am in love with God.

6. "AFTER 37 YEARS" by Fred Tudors

My father abused my mom and my mom turned to drinking and abused me. It created resentment toward my father for the last 37 years. On my 10th birthday, my dad killed my mom's best friend and I harbored more resentments toward him. I didn't recognize evil emotions were controlling my life. I grew up without my father. I came to jail because someone shot my step-son and killed him. I was in retaliation mode. I finally forgave my father in order to move on from the original abuse and choices by my father. In my cell I asked God to forgive me and I was able to let go.

My time here in Colorado with my alcohol and drug addiction lead me to neglect my children. So I wrote to them and asked them to forgive me. My older son, 17 years old, is writing to me and he is more open to me. My younger son, 16 years old, is still upset with me. I let my kids down and I have failed them many times. Forgiving my father was like getting a big load off my back. I realized that my lifestyle was more like my father's: prison, drinking, drugs and violence. I want to break the cycle of addiction and abuse. That is what I am working on now. I don't want to be in bondage anymore.

7. "VICTIM TO VICTOR" by Georgette Wires

When I was a little girl, I was abused in every way possible. Being physically abused hurt me more on the inside than it ever could on the outside. It seemed the only "attention" I got was when I was being sexually abused. After a while that all became normal. So normal that by the age of ten I was being pimped out by my aunt. I remember being so scared the very first time but already I had developed the "people pleaser" mentality so I didn't want to make her mad. My mother was a disciplinarian and a workaholic so all the things that went on with me she never knew until 2007.

Debbie was supposed to be babysitting me not pimping me. After two years of this she introduced me to cocaine at the age of 12 which I would end up battling for the next 26 years. I was hitting the pipe with grown men who, in turn, began to use my body as their playground. Somewhere deep inside of me I knew all these things were wrong, but after awhile it all became twisted and I thought it was normal.

Growing up around pimps, hustlers, and drug dealers, it seemed my destiny to become a part of the streets. I didn't get tossed into them, they were embedded in me. All the while living a double life, because at home I was a daughter with no affectionate connection to my mother. I was teased at school in the projects because I was a half breed so, therefore, I was born a misfit. Not ever being able to fit in anywhere, only with my aunt and her "friends."

I was given up for adoption at birth because my biological mother got pregnant when she was underage. I battled the issue of abandonment for a long time. Somewhere throughout all this, my mom and my Grandma, and I went to church every Sunday. Once I began to get older and began to hear "God is love," "God loves you," "Jesus loves you." I remember questioning it because if He was near, why was my life so full of pain and hurt? Did He not like me either?

At 15, my dad passed, which didn't mean too much to me because he had done his damage too. When I was seven my dad moved his mistress into our home destroying everything my brothers and I knew to be normal. To this day I don't know how my mother came through and still remained sane. She took me and my brother Sam and moved out which opened the door for more abusers. Babysitters who would beat me crazy, one even burned my arm with scalding water. For whatever reason, I was always taught to believe that I was bad and unwanted. There were wounds that would scar me and become oppressive holds on me throughout life.

My mother and I moved to Colorado. Her cousin lived out here and they were "super sanctified." Something I didn't know about. They were strict, mean, and abusive, but "churchy." So, I went from playing the role of an adult from 10-15 and doing adult things, to no freedom, wearing dresses, being in church, and missing my home in Illinois. I was a sad fish out of water. I wasn't getting with the program due to "street mentality."

I once again got the hell beat out of me! It was so severe the neighbors called the police and when they came I told them I was alright because I didn't want to leave my mom. Well instead a short time later I met a pimp (how ironic) and ran away with him. Nobody ever came looking for me. I was with him three long months. Everything my aunt had taught me, the ante, just went up, because it went from bedrooms to street corners all across America. Then the beatings began and I didn't understand. So I ran away from him and made my way back to Colorado. My mama let me in, but to my surprise she never asked one question. I began to believe she didn't care.

Years later I figured out that she just simply didn't know how to care. After getting back here, I met a high-

The Ultimate Parenting Guide

profile hustler and he became my entire world until I got pregnant at 17. He got on cocaine and everything began to change. He began beating on me leaving and staying gone all the while making me believe it was because of me. After two babies, I entered prison at 20, took a 3 year sentence and turned it into 20 years. Through the next 20 years, I would enter prison, get out, after two weeks free I would relapse and be on the run, only to return back to prison. During my relapse, I would get involved with men who took abuse to a whole other level. I have been beat, burned, stabbed, and left for dead by men I thought loved me.

The abuse was normal to me because I didn't know anything else. To me it was love. All they had to do was say, "I love you" and they had me. My last relapse ended up being my worst (2007). I hated myself. I hated who and what I had become. I didn't want to go any farther. So I figured if I kill myself, I would be easing everybody's pain. Well, I didn't succeed and in my frustration of not being able to even do that right I began to cry out to God like I had never did before.

I knew about Jesus, even had a relationship with Him. He had a special kind of way of dealing with me. Only in jail would I seek him. He always made himself known to me, but when I got out of jail, I would leave him at the door. Never intentionally, of course. I wanted to know what was so wrong with me that I couldn't even get anything right! My life had become a series of failures. I couldn't begin to understand the way of it all.

If you don't know you are broken, how do you know you need to be fixed. Because of all that happened, I had developed deep wounds that over time had become buried. It seemed with each incident the scab would be pulled off and more salts would be poured into me. Pain that sometimes felt as if someone took my heart and decided to scrape it raw. How could I even begin to tell anyone what I was feeling when I couldn't describe it to myself?

A feeling of loss, hoping to be found but not knowing how to say help me. When it hurt, I would get high. When I got high, I would run and I ran right back to the arms of the streets where for some reason I felt accepted and wanted, only to quickly become a victim of more abuse. How does one become a mother of eight beautiful children and not even know how to mother them?

Here's a better question. How does one become an adult and not know how to function as an adult? Well, that was me and that was my story. All I felt was the hurt, pain and heartaches of the people that said they loved me. All I wanted to do was be that little girl again and run and hide somewhere I couldn't be found. But really, I wish somebody would have found me. I wish someone would even come looking for me. But for years and years no one ever came. As time went on either I found myself in the streets or in a jail cell.

All I wanted was someone's arms around me, someone to sit with me, and talk to me, letting me know they understood. For some reason everybody always thought I needed tough love. Today I disagree. Tough love, unfortunately was something I already knew. To me it says; lonely, outcast, you don't belong here, you are not good enough, you disgust me, beat me, hurt me, you don't deserve good things, you will never amount to anything! When people are in pain you don't beat and badger them down more. I was so out of touch, when my mother did try to reach me, I was too far gone. I had built a thick wall around my heart, not even realizing it or knowing the how and why of it. I didn't even believe my own mother loved me.

Years later I come to realize if she never said it, her actions always spoke way louder. She always had my children and she never turned her back on me. I just didn't know how to say, "I'm so heart sick, and full of bullet holes."

Who can help me? Through the years, I learned that there is only one who could help me. His name is Jesus! And I only became acquainted with him in jail. One thing about him, he has never abandoned me. No matter what I've done or where I've been. Even when I left him behind, he is somebody that never gave up on me. At 15, I didn't understand who Jesus was and how he could be so gentle and kind. When I first began my walk with him, it was so lovely and nice I never wanted him to leave me. I didn't understand that in order for him to stay with me I had to stay with him.

I left him many times and each time my pains got worse and worse because now I had been introduced to guilt and shame. It made me sad even more so because I knew I had let him down. I had to learn that once you repent and ask for forgiveness, he is not like man, he really forgives you. He began to take each heartache, and the pain that was connected to it and started the healing process with each hurtful memory he took away the sting that was connected to it. All the while showing me the deeper meaning of forgiveness. Forgiving my abusers then forgiving myself. In that, freedom has come.

Sometimes the enemy will tap at me and begin to accuse me all over again. He will try and tell me how unworthy I am and all that comes with it. In my mind I have learned that, that is where the battle begins. The more I study God's Word, the more I have to fight with. Through all of my failures and all my falls, Jesus has been right there, with out stretched arms waving me back to him! With Him, I don't have to explain because he already knows about it. It is so much relief—just giving it all to him. After 17 years I finally understand that he wanted a surrendered heart — my heart where my free will lies. All these years I had been saying, Lord I give you my life. Well I get it now, my life is something he already has.

When folks say walking with Jesus is a journey. It really is! I used to want everything right now. With Him, change doesn't happen in a right now way. With every fall, in my getting back up, I have learned something different every time. Most importantly, he will never leave me nor forsake me. He will come to me and not leave me an orphan. He is a true living God and his Word is living and powerful. Life with him just gets better and better, no matter how alone I may feel, no matter how dark it may get, and no matter how strong the storm I know he is there. His love holds me, surrounds me and encourages me and all that I've gone through is just the preparation for His purpose in my life. *Romans 8:28* says, *"And we know that in all things God works for the good of those who love him, who have been called according to his purpose."*

And yes, we are all called no matter where you have been, who you are, or even where you come from. Our lives have purpose and meaning all with God getting the glory. Please don't give up and definitely don't quit. The greater the struggle, the greater the triumph. The power of Jesus Christ knows no limitations. My sins, my failures, and my mistakes are somehow weaved into the tapestry of my life and God makes no mistakes. He loves us all, one and the same. His mercy and compassion are truly real and he never changes. He really is the same today, tomorrow and for ever. Please open your hearts and call on him. He will answer and he is already waiting. Jesus loves you.

8. "I HAVE FORGIVEN MYSELF" by Teri Smith

I grew up being told I would never be anything. I was neglected, abandoned and belittled by my parents. I grew up feeling unworthy of love from anyone. I was very confused about who I was and I didn't like being in this world. I was sad and depressed as a child and experienced a lot of pain.

Feeling unimportant to my parents and felt like more of a burden to them and my grandparents.

I started using drugs and alcohol to help me cope with my self-hatred. It only increased as the guilt and shame consumed me. I came to a point in my life that felt like more than I could endure and tried many times to take my life. I always loved God and Jesus. The fear of hell, I believe kept me alive.

My alcohol use became an addiction and it got me in a lot of trouble. I have had to spend time in jail due to drinking and driving. I believe that saved my life. I had to forgive myself and allow the crucifixion of Jesus to be my source of surrendering.

As long as I continue to surrender my flesh and my heartaches to Jesus, I can feel the peace overcome the pain. I have forgiven myself for all the pain I have caused others in my life or the blood that Jesus shed for me is shunned and denied. The self forgiveness has allowed me to love myself for the first time and brought me healing and deliverance from alcoholism and suicidal thoughts.

Chapter 3

Reflections and Healing

1. Afflicted Adult Children

The world will be a better place if we can all learn from our parents' mistakes and not repeat them. But as it is, many people who don't have a good role model could make the same mistakes without realizing it. Therefore, it is very critical to process any hurts and pains that are caused by our parents' abusive behavior and destructive lifestyles. Until we take care of our wounds, we cannot provide a nurturing and caring environment for our children. What we need to do is recognize our weaknesses and make changes to be a better parent. Once you recognize where you have been, you can become more equipped to deal with your pain and make necessary changes. The following reflection can help you to see where you have been and how you are affected by it.

Questions for Reflection:
1. While you were growing up, were you a happy and content child or unhappy and miserable at home?
2. How was your relationship with your parents?
3. What were their positive influences?
4. Did your parents have faith in God? If they did, did they teach you about God?
5. What were their weaknesses and mistakes?
6. What was missing in their parenting?
7. What did you want from your parents?
8. What kind of bad habit(s) did you inherit from your parents?
9. What kind of parent do you want to be?

10. What do you want your children to remember about you?
11. What do you want your children to remember about your faith?
12. How's your relationship with your parents now? Do you have any issues that need to be resolved?

Find out if you are a wounded adult child.
What were your responses to the questions above? Are there any areas that you need to experience emotional healing? If you don't feel like you have things to honor about your parents, you may still have some issues that you need to take care of. Adult children who have not taken care of their childhood problems have a difficult time being positive role models for their children.

My Reflections:

1. While you were growing up, were you a happy and content child or unhappy and miserable at home? — I was not a happy child, I lived in fear because of my father's drinking problem and his hot temper. He beat my mother and that was a horrifying experience for me. He was harsh to my older brother as well and it was very difficult for me to forgive him.

2. How was your relationship with your parents? — I didn't have any problems with my mother but she was gone a lot and I didn't have a close relationship with her. After I left home and I had my own family, I was able to spend more time with her while I was attending the seminary and I then developed a close relationship with her. I didn't have a good relationship with my father. He hated me because I would tell him to stop being abusive to my mother and my older brother. I had a difficult time forgiving him. Eventually God helped me to forgive my father after he had died.

3. <u>What were their positive influences</u>? — My mother sent me to church and helped me to strengthen my faith in God. My father was very destructive and abusive when he drank. He taught me the destructiveness of drinking so I decided not to touch alcohol.

4. <u>Did your parents have faith in God? If they did, did they teach you about God</u>? — My mother had faith in God but my father didn't. My mother helped me to have more trust in God by praying for me when I was struggling with nightmares and headaches. She has been a very positive influence in my journey of faith. I learned that people with faith can handle problems of life much better than people who don't have faith in God. My mother took me to many revival meetings and that helped me to grow spiritually. From time to time, she shared her story of faith and how God has helped her at different times and that was helpful to me.

5. <u>What were their weaknesses and mistakes</u>? — My father was not a nurturing father. He was critical and a violent person. He didn't give us a chance to reconcile when he committed suicide. His death affected my whole family in a negative way and still some of our family members can't talk about it. They haven't processed their pain caused by our father's suicide. My mother was a strong woman but she loved my father too much and she stayed in the marriage even though I told her to divorce him.

6. <u>What was missing in their parenting</u>? - My father didn't live out his faith so he didn't have God's values. He was lacking in self-control, understanding and compassion for his family. Our suffering was caused by his actions, but he didn't realize it. My mother endured so much pain for the sake of their marriage. She should have been more understanding of how much her children suffered at home by watching our father beat her.

7. <u>What did you want from your parents</u>? — I wanted my

The Ultimate Parenting Guide

father to be loving and not violent. I wanted a loving relationship with my father. I wanted to show him how much I cared for him but I couldn't do that when he was alive. I wanted my mother's time and attention more when I was growing up, but she was trying to bring food to the family so I understood it. I am thankful that I was able to get to know her later.

8. What kind of bad habit(s) did you inherit from your parents? — My father didn't have much patience and I don't have much patience either. I have to work hard in that area and I am learning to pray to God for wisdom to deal with other people who are inconsiderate. My mother's calmness in dealing with others has helped me a lot.

9. What kind of parent do you want to be? — I want my children to know that I love them and care for them. I want to be their cheerleader. I want to be the most encouraging person in their lives so they can understand God's unconditional love for them.

10. What do you want your children to remember about you? — I want them to know that I tried my best to love and care for them as a mother even though I wasn't always available for them.

11. What do you want your children to remember about your faith? — I want them to know that God was with me and I lived a full life by loving and serving God. I want them to know that I cared about their relationship with God, their spiritual growth and that I prayed for them.

12. How's your relationship with your parents now? Do you have any issues that need to be resolved? — I was able to resolve my resentment toward my father and forgave him with God's help. I have processed all of the hurts caused by my father. I have a close relationship with my mother. I am thankful that she is still alive and I can show her how much I care for her.

Reflections and Healing

2. Processing Hurts and Pains

If you had problems with your parents, I encourage you to follow this exercise to experience healing.

1. Repentance

Adult children who are not living with their parents are grown up, and are removed from the abusive situation. But if they keep holding onto bitterness, they are continuously letting themselves be abused emotionally and mentally not by the person who abused them, but by their own unforgiving heart.

An unforgiving heart will open the door for the devil to come in and put you in a prison of bitterness and anger. As long as a person justifies holding onto anger, they are choosing to be victims of the past. They cannot function and are immobilized with pain. Therefore, they cannot be a nurturing parent because they are wounded and choose to live in that condition of hurt and pain.

Many are in the prison of bitterness even after they are freed from the environment of abuse. That's what I am trying to address here so you can learn to forgive and let go of painful memories and be free from a spiritual prison.

Write a confession letter to God. Go back to your childhood and don't focus on others but your own sin and ask for forgiveness one by one. Confess your sins: *"If we confess our sins, he is faithful and just and will forgive us our sins and purify us from all unrighteousness."* (1 John 1:9) *"For I will forgive their wickedness and will remember their sins no more."* (Hebrews 8:12)

As you reflect on your life, you will see things more

clearly and you will develop more compassion for others. Those who are carrying a heavy burden of anger have a big file cabinet in their mind that have many people's names and events that they cannot let go of. Put a "mental garbage can" next to you. This garbage can has a lid. One by one, as you ask for forgiveness and forgive others, put them in your mental garbage can and shut the lid.

Continue this process until you cannot think of any more sin. Then ask the Holy Spirit for help.

Prayer: "Lord Jesus, I have made a decision to forgive everyone who has sinned against me, especially my parents. I have let go of all the resentment, anger, bitterness and hate that I have carried for so long. Please forgive me. I ask you to give me a new heart. Bless me with your wisdom, knowledge, understanding, revelation, compassion and mercy. I ask you to heal my memory so I can move on with my life and I can teach my children about your love through my love for them. Please help me find peace with you, peace with myself and others, especially with my parents. I pray this in Jesus' name. Amen."

2. Write a letter of forgiveness

You can tell God that you forgive your parents for anything they did wrong, one by one. You can also write a letter of forgiveness to your parents, but don't list all the sins they committed. Just tell them that you have been hurt but you have forgiven them.

If you don't feel you want to send out the letter, don't do it. Wait until you are ready and when God asks you to, then send it. If you are not sure how they will react to your letter or if there is a small voice telling you not to send it out, don't send it out. God may be telling you that the letter will only hurt someone even though you might have good intentions.

You can get hurt more if your parents don't think they

did anything wrong. Pray and ask God for wisdom before you send out the letter. In some cases, it's better not to even mention that you forgive them. They might become defensive and say you were bad and they treated you justly.

People who hurt others usually don't know that they are hurting them. They justify their sin and they think others deserve punishment. Remember, you could be that person as well, so you need God's wisdom.

3. Write a letter of gratitude (85% and 15%)
People who have been bombarded with bad memories about their parents are blinded in the areas of seeing good things in their parents. Not everyone is completely bad or evil. We are all created in the image of God, there is good in all of us even though we may not see it.

I think everyone has 85% of God given goodness in them and 15% of weakness and dark side where we can make mistakes and fall into sin.

Try to see their good side which you may have forgotten about or taken for granted. Write down all the good things your parents did for you as you were growing up. If you can, send them a letter of appreciation for being your parents and bringing you into the world without mentioning any of their mistakes.

Everyone has good qualities, and if we only see bad in others, then we have forgotten that they too are created in the image of God. How would you feel if others see only the bad part of you and continuously point fingers at you. If we are only thinking about our parents' faults, we may have to change our perception of others so we can learn to forgive.

People who have a problem seeing good in other people are critical people. These people only see bad in others and they become critical parents. They can destroy their children's confidence and will keep pointing at them, saying they are bad. Children need nurturing parents who can have compassion and a forgiving heart. Try to develop a grateful heart to save yourself and your children so you don't destroy their spirit and life with a critical, judgmental and negative spirit.

What you need is the fruits of the Holy Spirit developing in your heart so you can bless your children with the same seed to see their fruits. Paul wrote, *"But the fruit of the Spirit is love, joy, peace, patience, kindness, goodness, faithfulness, gentleness and self-control. Against such things there is no law. Those who belong to Christ Jesus have crucified the sinful nature with its passions and desires. Since we live by the Spirit, let us keep in step with the Spirit."* (Galatians 5:22-25)

Meditate on the words: love, joy, peace, patience, kindness, goodness, faithfulness, gentleness and self-control. Which area do you need to work on to teach your children that you are walking with the Holy Spirit?

Prayer: "Lord Jesus, help me to plant the good seed in my children's heart so they can learn to follow the Holy Spirit's leading in their life. Bless me so that I will be the most encouraging, comforting, nurturing, and loving parent to my children. Bless them so they can bless others with your help."

4. If you can, contact your parents for reconciliation

If you are an adult child and you are still hurting, you may need to initiate reconciliation by approaching your parents with gentleness and kindness.

First, tell them you love them and care for them, and that you have been carrying a big load for a long time. It's time for you to let it go because you value your relationship with them. You can also ask them to forgive you of your mistakes and tell them you forgive them of their mistakes also.

Ask the Lord if you really need to do this. If He says you should, then approach them, but ask the Lord to give you the right words so it will be a beneficial meeting for both you and your parents. Paul wrote, *"If it is possible, as far as it depends on you, live at peace with everyone." (Romans 12:18)*

5. When reconciliation doesn't work

When you try to communicate with your parents that you are hurting because of their mistreatment of you in the past, some parents might recognize their fault and you may be able to talk it out and resolve it.

For some parents, however, they cannot admit that they made a mistake. Instead of admitting their fault, they may think you are attacking them. When that happens, just let it go and be glad that you are an adult and that you don't have to live with them. Just don't put yourself in an abusive situation anymore. Try to work on relationships now so you don't carry resentment or get hurt any more.

If you cannot have a close relationship with your parents because they don't want the relationship, you tried your best and you have to rest in that. Some relationships don't work out because you constantly get hurt by the porcupine personalities they have.

Those who have been around porcupine people can become like them if they don't realize what they are influenced by. So make sure you don't act out the way they do, or say the things they do.

6. If you still can't forgive

One day a woman asked me to anoint and pray for her so God would take away her anger. I asked her, "Are you willing to forgive everyone that hurt you?" She told me she wasn't willing to do that. She just wanted God to do it for her. I told her, "God cannot take away your anger until you are willing to make a decision to forgive. So, what you need to do is to start repenting first." She couldn't understand what I was saying. Why would she need to repent when other people did wrong?

What other people did to her was wrong but her part is to forgive and let it go. I explained to her that holding on to resentment and anger is sin. Jesus gave us clear direction on what to do with our hurts and pains.

Jesus said, *"But I tell you who hear me: Love your enemies, do good to those who hate you, bless those who curse you, pray for those who mistreat you."* (Luke 6:27-28)

The reason we don't have peace in our heart is because we are not obeying the Lord. I am not saying this to those who are living in a constantly abusive situation. If you are living in an abusive and violent situation, and continue to be beaten and hurt, you need to pray for wisdom so you can somehow stop the abuse. If you can't stop the abuse, you might have to ask for outside help. If that doesn't work, you might have to remove yourself from that situation. When the abuse stops, then you can think about how you can forgive and let go of anger and resentment.

Jesus said, *"And when you stand praying, if you hold anything against anyone, forgive him, so that your Father in heaven may forgive you your sins."* (Mark 11:25) God is not going to forgive your sins unless you forgive others. *"Do not judge, and you will not be judged. Do not condemn, and you will not be condemned. Forgive, and you will be forgiven."* (Luke 6:37) Read the following Scripture to learn which area you need to work on so you can forgive.

"Who is wise and understanding among you? Let him show it by his good life, by deeds done in the humility that comes from wisdom. But if you harbor bitter envy and selfish ambition in your hearts, do not boast about it or deny the truth. Such 'wisdom' does not come down from heaven but is earthly, unspiritual, of the devil. For where you have envy and selfish ambition, there you find disorder and every evil practice. But the wisdom that comes from heaven is first of all pure; then peace-loving, considerate, submissive, full of mercy and good fruit, impartial and sincere. Peacemakers who sow in peace raise a harvest of

righteousness." (James 3:13-18)

Prayer: "Lord Jesus, help me to see the big picture so I can see what you see. Help me to have spiritual discernment so I can see why I cannot forgive. Wash me with the blood of Jesus Christ and set me free from the prison of bitterness. Help me to obey you and forgive everyone. I have made a decision to forgive everyone. Heal my broken heart and let me have the peace that comes from you."

7. No one is perfect

We all make mistakes, but recognizing our mistakes is important. Many abusive people, however, don't see how much they are damaging others. They justify their sin and their perception is corrupt. That's why we need God's values — love God and love others. Children are an easy target since they cannot defend themselves and some parents act like bullies. Don't be like them. We need God's wisdom to deal with bully parents, and in some cases, if they don't change their attitudes and behaviors, you should limit how much time you spend with them so you can manage your hurts and pain.

If your parents do not have God's values and do not see the whole picture, they may deny hurting you. If that happens, let it go and don't try too hard to make them realize how they made a mistake. Pray for them and love them and treat them with respect as parents.

Jesus prayed for those who were crucifying him. *"Jesus said, 'Father, forgive them, for they do not know what they are doing.'" (Luke 23:34)*

Prayer: "Lord Jesus, help me to resolve all the issues that are heavy in my heart, especially my relationship with my parents. Please forgive my parents for what they have done. I forgive them. Help me to be a loving parent so I will be able to teach my children how to love and forgive. Help me to love and respect my parents. Transform my heart so I can be a good role model for my children to follow so they can learn to forgive."

8. Let go of your expectations (5% and 85%)

Many of our problems start with our unrealistic expectations of what other people should be doing for us. Also, we don't focus on what we can give, but what we can get. That's where our disappointment and discouragement starts.

I think people can only give 5%, but most people expect 85%. This creates a lot of resentment and anger because people's expectations are much higher than what people can give. Your parents gave you 5% and that's all they were able to give, so let go of your resentment. They tried their best—5% and you are expecting 85%. If you are still grieving over what you didn't get from your parents, you need to let go of your expectations.

What you may not realize is that as a child you were only able to give 5%. Your parents may have been expecting you to give them 85%. Give them a break and give yourself a break by forgiving them and forgiving yourself!

The Lord teaches us how to forgive by being an example for us. God knows we can't save ourselves with our own righteous actions. We just can't do it. He prepared a way for us to be saved. Jesus died on the cross for our sins. All we have to do is accept God's grace and what Jesus has done for us so we can be forgiven. Remember you need to be generous with what you have received—forgiveness from the Lord. Forgive your parents and forgive yourself.

Paul wrote, *"For all have sinned and fall short of the glory of God, and are justified freely by his grace through the redemption that came by Christ Jesus." (Romans 3:23) "Therefore, there is now no condemnation for those who are in Christ Jesus, because through Christ Jesus the law of the Spirit of life set me free from the law of sin and death." (Romans 8:1-2)*

Reflections and Healing

3. Rebellious Children

1. Weeping for your children

If your children are living in sin and they have turned away from the Lord, it's time to weep for your children and pray for God's mercy so He can help them. On the way to the cross, Jesus gave directions on what parents need to do. *"Jesus turned and said to them, 'Daughters of Jerusalem, do not weep for me; weep for yourselves and for your children.'" (Luke 23:28)* Ask God for mercy so He can bring healing in your children's hearts so they can turn to the Lord and live a godly life.

Prayer: "Lord Jesus, I ask for your mercy for my children so their hearts will be opened to see their spiritual condition. I pray for the spirit of repentance for my children and also for myself. If there is any sin I have committed against you and against my children, please forgive me. Help me to make things right with you and my children. I ask for your compassion for my family. Please speak to my children today so they can understand how much you love them and also understand what is right and wrong. Convict them of their sin so they can turn to you for forgiveness and change their lifestyle. Help me to make things right. I proclaim victory in Christ that my children will learn to fear the Lord, to love God, love themselves and love others."

2. Ask for a big picture

If you have already been weeping and praying for a long time, and do not have any idea why your children are turning their back against the Lord and are living in sin; it's time to ask God for wisdom and understanding so you will see the big picture, and find direction on what to do to help them and find peace.

Prayer: "Lord Jesus, help me to trust you and to know that you see the big picture. Help me to let go of my worries and fear about my children because you are with them. Please forgive them and have mercy on them. Reveal to them your purpose for their life."

3. Reflection

When our children sin, we first need to go to God and ask Him if there is any sin that we need to repent of. Many times we are not aware of our sin even though we try our best. God gave me understanding of why our children had problems and I contributed to a large portion of it. I was a lukewarm Christian so I wasn't able to teach my children the most important thing in the world: how to love God and serve Him. I wasn't a good role model even though I thought I tried my best.

Prayer: "Lord Jesus, please help me to understand if there is anything I need to change in my parenting. Please give me wisdom to understand why my children are rebellious. Help me to have the wisdom and power to make changes. If I did anything that was not right, please help me to understand so I can make it right."

4. A generational curse?

Children can learn from their parents' bad and ungodly habits. Many ungodly and destructive habits can be inherited if they don't reflect and see the destructiveness of what they are doing. Some people believe that this is a generational curse. Yes, the Scripture talks about generational curses and blessings. *"You shall not bow down to them or worship them; for I, the LORD your God, am a jealous God, punishing the children for the sin of the fathers to the third and fourth generation of those who hate me." (Deuteronomy 5:9)*

Jesus broke the curse. Paul wrote, *"Christ redeemed us from the curse of the law by becoming a curse for us, for it is written: 'Cursed is everyone who is hung on a tree.'"* (Galatians 3:13) God's grace covers everyone who seeks His forgiveness. Therefore, I don't believe some families have more of a curse than others. Some families may have developed ungodly destructive habits and they have justified their sinful actions and behaviors. We need to realize the destructiveness of our parents' mistakes and reject those mistakes for they do not help us live a godly life. We need to follow God's ways to find peace and to live a fruitful life.

Jesus can help us break the cycle of destructive habits if we only follow the Lord's commandments of loving the Lord and our neighbors. You must love yourself if you want to love your neighbors and loving yourself is to live a godly life. Also, we need to love our family and pay attention to them before we can truly love other people.

Paul said, *"If anyone does not provide for his relatives, and especially for his immediate family, he has denied the faith and is worse than an unbeliever."* (1 Timothy 5:8)

5. Influences beyond our control

We also need to remember that godly parents don't always produce godly children. There are many influences that affect our children and they have the responsibility of making their own decisions when they reach the age of accountability and no longer pay attention to their parents.

Children are affected by many influences: (1) Our culture and society where they grow up. Culture can have good values but without God, there is lack of good moral values which can influence them to justify sin and live an ungodly life. (2) Sinful nature plays a big role in children's rebellion and they may not have any respect for anyone including God's values. (3) The devil plants the seed of deception into people's hearts and tries to make people turn away from the Lord and be disobedient to their parents. (4) Friends who do not have God's high moral values can influence our children. (5) Ignorance and immaturity also play a big role even with people with good intentions.

That's why it's important to teach God's values when children are young, so that when they get older, they can resist the worldly, sinful and destructive values.

Even those who grew up with God's values don't always hold on to them because by the time they grow up, the world's influences can swallow their values and they may think what is bad in the eyes of God is good because the culture accepts them.

Don't lose heart when that happens: You have to keep planting the seed and praying for them so they can repent and follow the Lord someday.

We cannot always see the fruits the way we want to see them but parents have the responsibility of providing a loving and nurturing environment and to teach them how to love God and live a godly life. You will have more of a chance of seeing good fruits if you continuously plant the good seeds through nurturing your relationship with your children and praying for them.

6. Have you justified your temper or violent behavior?

Some parents focus only on children's destructive behaviors and not their own destructive behaviors which contribute to their children's rebellion.

One day I had a dream about a person who had a problem with having a hot temper. I heard him crying out, "Help me, help me." This person was wrapped in a blanket and plastic outside. When I removed the wrapping, his body was cut open in half and I saw the organs of his body. It was a terrible sight. No wonder this person couldn't help. I felt hopeless and helpless. I couldn't help him either because this person was beyond repair. When I woke up the Lord gave me understanding of the dream.

People who give themselves to anger and violence: (1) Accept the devil's lies that they have the right to be angry. (2) Can fall into sin by holding that anger in. (3) Justify their sin and turn to violence. (4) Don't try to change their behaviors. That's why you need to preach about forgiveness. Without forgiveness, there is no way a person can be free from the prison of anger."

Ask your children to forgive you and forgive yourself. Make changes so that you can learn to control your anger or violent behaviors. If you are a victim of violence, work on your forgiveness. Holding anger in is sin. *"'In your anger do not sin': Do not let the sun go down while you are still angry, and do not give the devil a foothold."* (*Ephesians 4:26*) Ask forgiveness from all the people you have hurt if you can.

7. Be gentle with yourself

Even though you may have tried your best and taught your children to follow God's values, your children still can turn out to be rebellious and walk on the path of destruction. Some children develop a bad habit of addiction and even though they know that they are wrong, they don't know how to let go of their destructive habit of an ungodly lifestyle.

You should not beat yourself up but continuously pray to God to help them turn around. God transformed many people in the Bible such as Moses, David and Paul. God is so mighty that He not only transformed their lives but used them to help others. We should never give up praying.

Be gentle with yourself when your children and grandchildren don't turn out to be God fearing people. What they need is your love, and if you can convince them that you love them, you will have more of a chance of helping them grow in faith. You can make a difference in your children's life if you can maintain a healthy relationship with your children and your grandchildren. You will have more of a chance of seeing good fruits if you continuously plant the good seeds through nurturing your relationship with your children and praying for them. Adult children continuously need their parents' love, affirmation and good role models. We may not always see the good fruits the way we want to see them, but still parents can have a long lasting positive effect on their children.

Don't be discouraged. Find out what God can do through you, through the prayer and the wisdom God gives you to make changes in the areas that you need. That's why it's important to plant God's values in your children when they are young to help them build a foundation of faith and good moral values. When they have God's values, they can resist worldly, sinful and destructive desires.

8. Do you love God more than your children?

Sometimes our problem with our children can start with us because we put our children before God instead of loving the Lord first. We may be loving our children more than God.

I had met a woman who lived in fear all the time because she thought something would happen to her children. She believed in God but she was not putting God first, but her children instead. Her fear was caused by not trusting God. We need to find out how much attention we give to our children. How do you measure it? Find out how much time you spend on praying or reading the Bible or prayer. If you don't focus on God and His greatness and grace to help your children, you are not relying on Him to help you and your children. Your love for the Lord is measured by how much time you spend with Him and by focusing on Him and by loving God for what He has done for you and what He can do for you.

The Scripture says, *"Love the Lord your God with all your heart and with all your soul and with all your mind and with all your strength." (Mark 12:30)* This Scripture is not telling you that you should not love your children. You should love your children, but you have to love God first and more than your children. If you put your children before God, you cannot have peace because your priorities are mixed up.

9. Children also have the responsibility

By the time children leave home or even before they leave home, if they start making decisions for themselves and go against their parents' godly advice, they are responsible for their sinful behaviors. Many godly parents grieve and live in guilt and shame when their children make mistakes. If you made mistakes, work on repair and do not give up hope.

Prayer: "Lord Jesus, help me to love you with all my heart, mind, soul and strength. Help my children to do the same. If I have sinned against you and my children, please help me to know what it is. Help me not to repeat the same mistake. Help me not to hurt my children any more. Help me to ask them for forgiveness and repair our relationship. Forgive me if I have contributed to my children's lack of faith or lack of godly character. Please bless them with a new heart and bring healing to their hearts."

10. Proclaim victory

Whenever you think about your children and are worried, proclaim victory in their lives in the name of Jesus until you find peace. "I proclaim victory in Jesus Christ that my Lord Jesus will help my children. My children will learn to understand God's love and they will learn to love God. My children will be surrounded with godly people. My children will hear God's clear voice. My children will be saved by the grace of God. I proclaim victory that I will be a parent that God wants me to be. My children will be glorifying God."

The Ultimate Parenting Guide

Reflections and Healing

4. Suffering from Regrets?

If you know that you are the one who messed up your children's lives because of your sin and destructive behaviors or addictive lifestyle, it's time to ask God to help you progress through the following steps.

1. Confession

One by one, ask God to forgive all the things you did or didn't do, that hurt your children. Write a confession letter to God and ask Him for forgiveness. You don't need to show this to anyone but tear it up and throw it away after you ask God for forgiveness. Prayer: "Lord Jesus, I have sinned against my children and hurt them. Please forgive me and help them to forgive me. Help heal our broken relationship and help me to build up our relationship with your love, wisdom and power."

2. Ask for healing

Ask the Lord how you can reconcile with your children. Prayer: "Lord Jesus, please teach me how to repair my relationship with my children. Give me your wisdom and discernment so I can help them process their pain. Help me not to repeat the same mistakes. Help me to understand their pain and help them to understand my deep regrets and how sorry I am."

3. Make a list

Make a list of the things you think you can do to reconcile and repair the relationship with them. Prayer: "Lord Jesus, bless me with ideas on how I can be a blessing to my children and help them see and feel my love and care for them." See if the list you made is realistic to you or not. Ask other mature Christians who can give you some honest feedback on what you should do to heal your broken relationship with your children.

4. Actions

Talk to your children or write a letter to ask them to forgive you. Prayer: "Lord, Jesus, please help me to explain to my children how truly sorry I am. Please open their hearts so they can forgive me. Help me so that I will not hurt them anymore with attitudes, words and actions."

5. Ask your children

If you can, write to them and ask them how you can make up for your mistake to ease their pain so they can let go of their resentment, anger, bitterness, and hate toward you. Prayer: "God, I am so sorry that I hurt my children. Please help my children to understand me and forgive me. Help me so I will be a blessing to them."

6. Resolution

If your children are not ready to talk to you or they don't respond to you, just pray for them. Forgiveness is a process. They may have forgiven you of your sins 1% today, but they have to do it in their own time. If you keep communicating with them how sorry you are, they may be able to forgive you 2% more tomorrow. If you hurt them again, you will lose what you have gained so keep your words.

7. Be realistic

If you are incarcerated, just asking for forgiveness may not be enough. It will take time. When you get out show them that you truly feel bad about what you have done by showing them that you have changed. Don't be discouraged if they forgive you only 10 % or 20%. Remember that your words can mean only so much. Words are great and we can tell them we have changed, but people are not convinced by words but by actions. Prepare to show them that you are going to be their blessings, not just with words, but also by actions.

Prayer: "Lord Jesus, please help me to keep my words that I will not hurt my family anymore with destructive behaviors. Help me to prove to them that I do care. Bless me with a gentle and nurturing spirit."

8. Ask the Holy Spirit

Prayer: "Holy Spirit, is there anyone else I have hurt because of my ungodly thoughts, words and actions. Please forgive me. Help me to love Jesus with pure love, a clear conscience and faith. Help my children to see how much you have helped me in my healing process. I ask for blessings of reconciliation with my family and with everyone."

9. Remember

There are times that you may think you need to contact someone to ask for forgiveness but in reality, if they don't want anything to do with you, then you should not contact them. If you have a restraining order, do not break the law but let it go by writing a letter of confession, tearing it up and throwing it in the garbage with prayer that God will do the rest. Keep praying so that God will help your children to forgive you.

Chapter 4

40 Parenting Tips

Parenting is a difficult task and we only have a few role models — our parents — who didn't know much about parenting and perhaps made many mistakes without even realizing it.

Many adults do not function properly in life because of the childhood trauma that was caused by their parents or others who assumed the role of their parents. Sometimes those who have been raised in a good Christian home are not ready to deal with life and have not learned the basics of how to love God, love themselves and love others.

How can we instill in our children God's values and morals and prepare them to deal with life? How can we help them to lead a life that will please God, and be productive in the community?

One way of learning how to be an effective parent is to learn from others' mistakes and success. The following lessons are what I have gathered from my own personal experiences and from my ministry. ACDF saints have also shared their thoughts and experiences of parenting in the section, "Adult children's comments."

1. Teach them about faith

Why do we need to be intentional about raising our children to grow in faith in God? What's the advantage of having faith? Children who have grown up having faith have many advantages in life. I will list some benefits and positive sides of helping your children to grow in faith.

(1) Faith gives them life tools: When you help your children

to grow with faith and have a relationship with God, you are giving them the most powerful and precious gift and the tools in life which can impact the rest of their lives. Having faith in Jesus not only saves their souls but gives them a solid foundation. They have someone to rely on besides you. They have someone to trust besides you. Many children want their parents' presence especially if they had a close relationship with their parents. Parenting is a temporary assignment. Your influences on your children are limited, but God is there with them all the time.

(2) <u>Faith gives children answers for life's questions</u>: People, even parents, don't have all the answers for why we exist and why we are here. Lack of direction and an unclear picture of why they exist can haunt them and even lead them to despair when they face difficulties in life. People with faith depend on God for answers as to why we exist. He blesses us with wisdom from the Bible and shows us how to focus on the positive aspects of life. The Bible gives us wisdom and answers, which other books do not.

(3) <u>Faith gives children strength in times of grief and loss</u>: People who have faith can handle grief and loss better than those who don't have faith. God has plans for eternity. These plans include the hope of seeing those who have gone on before us. Your children need to hear this so they can find comfort and strength in God even when they lose their loved ones. Also, God will always be with us when we lose others. People who are stricken by grief and loss can be immobilized with pain. God can heal them from a broken heart so they can cope with life having hope and dreams for the future.

(4) <u>Children with faith can have high values</u>: Children who grew up with good morals have more consideration of others because God has much higher moral values than cultural or social values. This helps many people to stay

on the right path. It will keep them from getting into immoral practices or trouble. There is less addiction and immoral behaviors if one has God's high values. Much of our grief and trouble is caused by our lack of moral values and principals.

(5) <u>Children with faith can have God's wisdom</u>: People's wisdom is limited. Children with faith can pray and rely on God's unlimited wisdom. The Lord gives direction and guidance when we face crossroads and when we lack the wisdom to know what to do in difficult circumstances.

(6) <u>Having Faith in God will help fill an empty heart</u>: People who are surrounded with loving people and material possessions can still have an empty heart. God is the only one who can fill our empty spot because that is how He made us. Children need to learn that their relationship with God will help them fill their empty heart, not people or things.

(7) <u>They can learn to love with God's help</u>: Children can develop a loving attitude toward God, themselves and others. People who don't know how to love themselves and others can follow a destructive path and not care about anything or anyone including themselves.

(8) <u>They can become less selfish</u>: Children who have faith will be less selfish because God's word teaches us to go beyond ourselves and to take care of others who are in need. They are happier because they have a clear direction on how to live a life that will please God instead of only pleasing themselves.

(9) <u>They can have fellowship with other believers</u>: This is one of the benefits of having faith in God. Others who have the same faith and high moral values can mentor your children as you send them to church and surround them with godly people.

(10) <u>They can learn to forgive</u>: God forgives us and we are

The Ultimate Parenting Guide

told to forgive. Forgiveness prevents a lot of troubled hearts and sometimes harmful behaviors.

To develop faith, children need to have a knowledge of the Scriptures. Read the Bible to them whenever you can. Even five minutes a day can make a difference. Pray with them and help them to be surrounded with people who have a relationship with God. Write the Scriptures that you want them to learn on sticky notes and put them on the walls to help them to memorize them. You need to help them to cultivate a relationship with the Lord through prayer. Take your children to church and surround them with people of faith. If you are not able to take your children to church, find others who can. Solomon, the wisest man in the world wrote, *"Train a child in the way he should go, and when he is old he will not turn from it."* (Proverbs 22:6)

Adult children's comments:
"My parents did a great job with my brother, sisters and I. They took us to church and sent us to school. They showed us that we had to do our chores, taught us how to love each other, and to share with the needy."

"I wish both of my parents would have continued to show and tell us more about God. Instead when we became older they let us make the decision whether we should attend church or not after our communion. I stopped attending church at the age of ten. That's when I was given the choice. I regret that I stopped attending."

"My faith has helped me to forgive myself and to let go of the past and my anger. It also gives me the will to worship and pray day and night to glorify Jesus Christ."

"My faith has helped me in my incarceration, knowing that God and His grace has been with me all these years. Without Him I would not be here, in jail, right now safe and getting clean."

"I did not know the love my parents had for each other. Jesus showed me how to love."

Prayer: "Lord Jesus, please help us to teach our children how important it is to learn about you. Surround them with godly people and protect them from the ungodly. Please help us to find the right church where our children can grow in faith. In Jesus name I pray. Amen."

2. Put relationship above rules and regulations

For some parents, keeping the rules is more important than their relationship with their children. These parents' love is related to how children perform. When children think parenting is all about just rules and regulations, they can and will rebel. They learn to hate authority because it represents to them harsh discipline with no mercy. They may think Christianity means rules and regulations. They have no clue that God really wants a loving relationship with them. Therefore, when they have a chance to make a decision, they quit going to church, thinking that they don't need any more rules.

It's very important to develop a loving relationship with your children so they can see that the reason you enforce rules and regulations is to help them grow. Children can misunderstand the reasons for rules and regulations. It's for them to be mature, avoid pit falls and troubles so they can live a peaceful and fulfilled life. We need to make sure that our children can understand that we love them. If our children know that we love them and that we want the best for them, they will be more open to listen to our suggestions.

Just making them follow the rules and regulations cannot give children good moral values. They need to be motivated by love and respect, not fear. They need to learn that their relationship with God and obeying His Word will give them clear direction on how to live a godly life and follow a peaceful path.

Prayer: "Lord Jesus, you died for my sins to forgive me. You have so much compassion and mercy. Help me to show my children mercy and compassion as you have shown me."

3. Understand your children are not perfect
Some parents are impossible to please because they have impossible standards. We need to be careful because children will give up trying. We need to make sure that we can recognize their best effort and encourage them instead of discouraging them. Some people expect their children to walk and run when their children can't even crawl. Here is where patience comes into play. Turn to the Scriptures. The Bible tells us that we all have sinned and we need God's grace to be saved.

The Lord knows that we are sinners and need forgiveness. He also knows that with a sinful nature and a desire for the world, we cannot live a perfect life. He provided a way for us to experience forgiveness. Jesus died for our sins. All we have to do is to believe in Jesus and ask for forgiveness. Even God provides a way to make us feel good by paving the way for forgiveness and salvation. We also need to make sure that our children know that we try to understand and forgive when they make mistakes.

Adult children's comments:
"My parents' expectations are for me to be perfect. I cannot be perfect."
"I would have liked for my mother to show me that she loved me, be understanding and caring, not judge me for everything."
Prayer: "Lord Jesus, is there anything that I need your forgiveness for in dealing with my children? Please help me to understand it so I can make changes. Help me to be gentle with my children when they make mistakes. Help me to

forgive them as you have forgiven me, so they can learn to forgive."

4. Practice what you preach

When parents live an ungodly lifestyle, display bad character, have a violent temper or live a destructive lifestyle, children do not have a good role model. Worse, some parents justify their violent behavior by saying that their children are bad and made them mad so they lost their temper. Actually what they need is self-control and learn how to solve problems peacefully. If children only see their parents losing their temper, they will assume that it's alright to lose their temper when things get tough. Also, this gives the message to children that their parents don't value them.

If any of your children are avoiding you or seem to hold any resentment or negative feelings toward you, don't let it go. Ask them kindly what is bothering them and try to amend the situation. Be willing to listen and try not to become defensive. Work on your listening skills. Children have the sense of justice and if you are hurting other members of the family, this can plant the seed of anger in other children as well. How you treat other family members will determine your relationship with everyone. Even if you didn't commit a sin against someone, that doesn't mean that it is okay. You need to have peace with God, peace within yourself and peace with everyone.

Prayer: "Lord Jesus, help me to be a good example for my children. Help me to understand my children as you understand them. Help me to see the goodness in them and not be critical of them when they make mistakes, as you have done with me."

5. Love them and make them feel special

Some children are starving for their parents' love and attention. Their parents don't know that children are like plants and are in need of watering and fertilizing in order for them to grow. When parents don't express how much they love them and nurture their children, these children will be searching for love somewhere else. Many times in the wrong places. Some may find love in God and stay on the course of faith, even though they don't have a close relationship with their parents. Many children, however, try to fill that empty hole with things like alcohol, drugs, violence, sex or other destructive behaviors.

Learn the language of love. Tell them how much you love them in different ways. Show them you love them by spending time with them. Develop a close relationship with your children by making an appointment with them and give full attention to each one of them individually. We need to make an intentional effort to make sure that our children know that we love them. You can also ask them how you can show them you love them. Children can teach us many things and they can teach us how to love them as well.

Treat your children with dignity, so they can learn to love themselves. Everyone is special in God's eyes, and you need to communicate that to your children with words and actions. You need to believe there is goodness in everyone, including your children, because everyone has inherited God's good characteristics. I believe everyone has 85% of goodness and 15% of weakness or sinful inclinations. If you have seen only badness in your children, you have missed God's image in them.

When you withhold basic needs such as food, clothing or love from your children as a way of punishment, you will be raising a child in a hostile environment where they will have a hard time trusting others, or to love and value themselves and life. God loves and values people. He gave His Son, Jesus, for us. Parents should communicate to their children that they are loved and valued.

Adult children's comments:

"My mother loved me and worked hard for me. She inspired me so much by being strong as a mother with my abusive step dad. She always prays for me when I'm gone and out doing wrong. Her prayer holds me every time I come home and I am blessed to be with her. This affected me knowing that no matter what I do or have done, it makes me feel special."

"I really appreciate the loving, devoted and loyal mother I was blessed with; and the loving, caring, and hard working father I was blessed with."

"My parents showed me love, affection, hugs, kisses... always goodnight kisses, and always made me feel safe. I had what I needed, food and clothing and they made sacrifices to move to a nicer house. They made me feel special and that helps me to know how to make my son feel special."

Prayer: "Lord, help me to love and show respect to my children, so they can learn to love and respect others as well. Help my children to understand how much I love them, so they can learn to love you, love themselves and love others. Help me to be a good example for my children. Help me to treat my children with your love and respect. Holy Spirit, guide my thoughts and actions so I can teach them how to make good choices. Bless and anoint me with the Holy Spirit and bless my children with the Holy Spirit so we can all live a life that will please you."

6. Teach them how to find friends with high moral values

From the time our children are little, we need to teach them the danger of following friends who do not have God's values. When they don't know who can help them live a godly life, they might follow ungodly people and a destructive path. Many children have no idea of the impact of being around others who have low or no morals. When pleasing these peers, they fall into destructive behavior. People who have low morals do not have any consideration of others. They have accepted worldly values which goes against God's values.

Many children are failing because they never were taught to find friends who have high moral values. Many children will listen to their friends more than their parents as they grow up. Therefore, it is essential to educate your children early on how to discern who has good moral values and who doesn't. Not all teenagers rebel, but there are some who do rebel. If you teach them to find godly friends, they might be able to avoid troubles. The worldly influence is so great. By the time they become teenagers, most of the time it is too late to teach them how to choose good friends.

Some children grow up in a Christian home and they seem to have good values, then when they leave home, they don't know how to avoid ungodly friends and unhealthy environments. They have no discernment to know how to avoid friends who will lead them in a destructive lifestyle. Their desires and worldly influences can swallow their values and they may think what is bad in the eyes of God is good because the culture accepts them. Their friends play a big role.

Paul warns, *"Do not be misled: 'Bad company corrupts good character.' Come back to your senses as you ought, and stop sinning; for there are some who are ignorant of God – I say this to your shame."* (1 Corinthians 15:33-34)

Prayer: "Lord Jesus, help my children to have wisdom to find good friends so they can walk a life of righteousness. Help them so they can shine your light on others but at the same time, help them avoid any friends with values that do not reflect your values."

7. Warn them of the dangers of addiction
Teach your children the danger of an addictive

lifestyle. Show them how drinking alcohol and using drugs is not only destructive, but also they are sin because it is misusing God's gift—gift of life and time. Many who do not understand the devastating effects of addiction fall into a destructive path and suffer from regrets in life.

"Do not set foot on the path of the wicked or walk in the way of evil men. Avoid it, do not travel on it; turn from it and go on your way. For they cannot sleep till they do evil; they are robbed of slumber till they make someone fall. They eat the bread of wickedness and drink the wine of violence." (Proverbs 4:14-17)

Give your children a tour of the places where people suffer from addiction. Have them watch educational movies and/or read books on the dangers of addiction. If you are suffering from addiction, you need to get help. You cannot expect your children to live a godly life if you are addicted to alcohol, drugs, violence or other destructive thoughts and behaviors. Many who are suffering from addiction will lose self-respect or end up incarcerated. We need to warn our children and teach them of all of the dangers of alcohol and drugs and how they play a big role in an ungodly lifestyle.

"Do you not know that your body is a temple of the Holy Spirit, who is in you, whom you have received from God? You are not your own; you were bought at a price. Therefore honor God with your body." (1 Corinthians 6:19-20)

Adult children's comments:

"Both of my parents were drug addicts and we did drugs together. There was something that was lost when that happened. I ended up losing respect for them and I ended up becoming an addict myself."

Prayer: "God help me to teach my children the danger of alcohol and drugs and anything that is going to hurt them. Please help me to be a good role model for them. Help me to be free from any kind of addictive thoughts or behaviors. Help me to have the strength to stay away from anything that is harmful for my mind, soul and body. Help me to guide my children to live a godly life. Please forgive my children and help them to repent if they live in sin and have addictive destructive lifestyles."

8. Avoid harsh discipline

Some parents use the Scripture to justify their violent behaviors. *"He who spares the rod hates his son, but he who loves him is careful to discipline him."* (Proverbs 13:24) I believe this Scripture has been misused by some parents who justify their violent temper toward their children.

What we need is God's wisdom so we can discipline our children without damaging their spirit and our relationship with them. We need to avoid any harsh discipline if it hurts them emotionally, mentally and/or physically. The focus should be on teaching them with love and patience what is right and wrong; not to hurt and terrorize them.

"Fathers, do not exasperate your children; instead, bring them up in the training and instruction of the Lord." (Ephesians 6:4) *"Fathers, do not embitter your children, or they will become discouraged."* (Colossians 3:21)

Anything that damages and discourages our children needs to be stopped and examined. Not only our behaviors, but our words, tone of voice, and attitude toward our children make a difference in their development and growth.

Many damaged and traumatized children come from violent homes where harsh punishment is accepted as a normal way of dealing with children. We can teach our children what is right and wrong without yelling, screaming, calling them names or hitting them.

There are many ways to make children grow and learn important lessons without hitting them and scaring them. Everyone makes mistakes and parents are no exception. If we learn how to talk and convince our children to obey and follow, this will help them learn how to solve problems in a non-violent way. Many children who grew up in fear of physical violence have had a difficult time holding their temper after they become parents. Many repeat the same violent behaviors their parents showed them.

Our attitudes, words and behaviors need to create an environment of love and understanding. Children who grow up beaten by their parents think violence is how to deal with their anger and frustration when their children do not act the way they want.

We can be firm and find a non-violent way of disciplining kids. Help them to follow your instruction with love, not fear. If fear is the main motivation, when there is no fear, then they can break the rules. Children who eventually grow up, have no fear of their physically weak parents. Fear doesn't work.

If you are screaming and yelling at your children, they may be doing the same thing to you someday. Some parents who beat their children end up being hurt when their children get older, bigger and stronger. When children see that the stronger will rule, when they become stronger they will try to rule over the weak.

Many children suffer from words that their parents have said, and from beatings they received, while they were growing up. Many are prisoners of hate and anger. We can avoid this grave mistake by talking with them and teaching them consequences.

The goal is to teach them and not repeat the same mistake, while building up relationships. Relationships based on fear will end up hurting many people. We need to teach our children how to be loving and respectful of each other even when our children make mistakes. Just because you were raised in a violent home, or your parents cursed at you, doesn't mean you have to repeat the same mistakes. Any way that you try to justify your sin and violent behavior, is what you need to stop and change.

Prayer: "Lord Jesus, help me to be gentle with my children when they make mistakes. Help me to forgive them as you have forgiven me, so they can learn to forgive."

9. Teach them to be generous

People tend to be selfish if they do not know what God wants them to do with their life. We should teach our children to have clear goals of serving the Lord according to His will.

Jesus gave us clear direction on what we need to focus on in life. We need to be disciples of Jesus and make disciples of Jesus. *"Then Jesus came to them and said, 'All authority in heaven and on earth has been given to me. Therefore go and make disciples of all nations, baptizing them in the name of the Father and of the Son and of the Holy Spirit, and teaching them to obey everything I have commanded you. And surely I am with you always, to the very end of the age.'" (Matthew 28:18-20)*

What the Lord wants for us is to use our gifts to serve others, not just ourselves and our family. I encourage you to spend 50% of your time and energy to serve your family and 50% to serve others. This will teach your children that there are things they need to do besides just serving themselves, that there are other people who need to be shown love.

Many people who fall into a destructive, selfish, sinful lifestyle, do not have a clear direction on which way to go. When we fail to teach children how to help others, their time and energy will be focused on being self-serving. Jesus came to give us life abundantly. This abundant life comes from finding and developing a close relationship with the Lord and obeying His command to reach out to the lost people and help needy people.

Again, just talking to them is not good enough. You need to show them that you practice what you preach. Volunteer to help with the soup kitchen for the homeless, big brothers, big sisters, habitat for humanity, visit nursing homes, serve in the food bank or get involved in prison ministry or any kind of ministry to serve others. Encourage your children to help others when they are young so they learn the value of helping and serving others.

Finding joy in serving others is something that many people don't know anything about. If you can teach your children to find joy in serving, you are helping them to find happiness. Donate to food banks and help the homeless; visit the nursing homes and try to have your children be involved so they can learn to help others. If you cannot afford to donate financially, volunteer your time.

Adult children's comments:

"My mother taught me to do the right thing and help people, even when the people don't pay you back or treat you right. Your reward comes from the Lord, not from other people. So no matter what other people do, as Christians we answer to God and do the right thing to please God. She did this in her actions and in life."

Prayer: "Lord Jesus, help me to teach my children how to help others. Help me to teach them how to share the good news of Jesus with others."

10. Avoid favoritism

There are many examples of how some parents showed favoritism, and this brings disasters into the family. Isaac favored Esau and Rebecca favored Jacob. Eventually the fight for their father's blessings caused Esau to have murderous thoughts, and Jacob had to run away from home.

Jacob didn't learn the destructiveness of favoritism and he repeated the same mistake. He made a colored coat for Joseph. Joseph's brothers were jealous and thought about killing him, but they sold him as a slave instead. Even though the end turned out good because Joseph forgave his brothers, Jacob suffered greatly because his sons told him that Joseph was dead.

Jacob's story teaches us that we need to treat our children the same, so we don't plant the seed of resentment and anger in our children's hearts. We can help their relationships by not comparing them or treating them differently. We need to teach our children how much we value them so they all feel special.

Teach your children to rejoice when others do well, especially their siblings. Don't ever make any comments that one sibling is doing better than the others. This creates jealousy and it is unhealthy. Everyone has different gifts and as parents we need to help them to recognize them and encourage them to use them.

Prayer: "Lord Jesus help me to treat all my children with love and treat them as you would want me to. Help me to make them feel special. Help me to teach them that they don't need to compete with each other because you have created them as unique individuals. Help them to see that you value them and I value them as well."

11. Treat your parents with love and respect

One of the ten commandments is to honor your parents. Are you an example for your children by showing respect to your parents? Don't expect your children to respect you, if you don't show respect to your parents.

"Children, obey your parents in the Lord, for this is right. 'Honor your father and mother' – which is the first commandment with a promise – 'that it may go well with you and that you may enjoy long life on the earth.'" (Ephesians 6:1-3)

Resolve any animosity you have with your parents, forgive them and maintain a good relationship so your children can see the goodness in your relationship. What we tell our children needs to be acted out so they can follow in your footsteps.

Be a good role model by treating your parents with love and respect and honor them whenever you can. Expect that your children will treat you just like you treated your parents. So, plant the good seed instead of the bad seed.

Prayer: "Lord Jesus, help me to love and respect my parents so that I can be a good role model to my children."

12. Teach them what it means to fear God

Some parents think that if their children have faith, they have fear of the Lord. That's not always true. We need to teach our children what it means to fear God. Webster's New World Dictionary describes fear as a feeling of anxiety and agitation caused by the presence or nearness of danger, evil, pain, timidity, dread, terror, fright, apprehension, awe and reverence. I think reverence is how I want to describe fear here.

Many people who have high moral values and live a godly life have learned to have reverence for the Lord. Solomon, the wisest man that ever lived said, *"The fear of the LORD teaches a man wisdom, and humility comes before honor."* (Proverbs 15:33) *"Through love and faithfulness sin is atoned for; through the fear of the LORD a man avoids evil."* *"Fear of man will prove to be a snare, but whoever trusts in the LORD is kept safe."* (Proverbs 29:25)

Giving God proper love and respect is fearing God. Teach children that they need to love the Lord more than anyone or anything. This is a simple statement, but it's hard for many people, even those who claim to have faith in God. The Scripture says, *"Love the Lord your God with all your heart and with all your soul and with all your mind and with all your strength."* (Mark 12:30)

Loving God is putting Him first in everything. Our focus, attention and devotion should be to read the word of God and to pray and obey the Lord, not just Sunday, but everyday and every moment. When our children forget this, they will put themselves, other people or things above God. The result will be a disaster. Children will see and learn from you, and you need to teach them to love the Lord first. Everyday, at least once a day, remind your children how good God is to them. We need to teach them a habit of recognizing the Lord's work and to praise Him. You have to be intentional about this so they can develop a habit of loving and thanking God in their lives.

Prayer: "Lord Jesus, help me to love you with all my heart, mind, soul and strength and help me to teach my children to do the same."

13. Teach them to manage their time

Our life is a gift from the Lord. Our life is the time we have on earth. We need to teach our children how to use their gift of life to glorify the Lord. Many people have not considered that their time is for the Lord. Many misuse their time, and gift of life, in things that do not have anything to do with their spiritual growth; just wasting away their gifts.

The more children watch TV and play video games, the more they are influenced by the world. Therefore, it's harder for them to develop God's values. The Lord's standards for living are much higher than the law. Children who believe in God and know the Bible should have higher moral values.

I heard a woman say that when she was growing up, she was allowed to watch TV one hour a day and a half hour to watch the News. This gave her more time to do some other constructive things, like reading good books.

Unless we teach our children how to manage time and take responsibility, they will be wasting their life away. They can be influenced by culture and social values, which don't always reflect God's moral values. That's one of the reasons why our children have a difficult time following the Lord. They have too many distractions and not enough time for the

Lord. Teach them how to manage their time wisely. How we spend our time reflects our faith and values.

Use every opportunity to explain God's Word and remind them that God can help them. Read them the gospels (Matthew, Mark, Luke and John) to teach them about Jesus whenever you can so they can develop a relationship with the Lord. Our life is for the Lord and to glorify Him. When we forget to teach this to our children, they will focus on something that will lead them to non-productive or destructive lifestyles. Also, have them involved in sports or groups where they promote good values like boy scouts or girl scouts etc.

Prayer: "Lord Jesus, teach me how to spend my time wisely so I can love you and give you glory every day. Help me to teach my children how to love and glorify you every day and they can be involved in good groups where they can learn good values."

14. Teach them how to grieve their losses

We need to teach our children that what we have received are all temporary gifts from the Lord. Our life, our time, our health, our finances, our family and our relationships are temporary gifts. They are not ours, but are used to give God glory. This is a very important lesson, but many forget about it, especially when they lose their loved ones.

How can we teach our children to be ready for the world — a world that we will continuously experience loss and grieve for people and things. Life is much more difficult when we don't understand the principal of ownership. The Lord has it all, and we are given the chance to enjoy His gifts for a while. When people don't learn this they get angry when they lose something or someone because they think they own them. They think God has taken them away.

What they don't realize is that they have received a

temporary gift and no one is going to have it forever. If they have a relationship with the Lord, that will help them with the process in times of grief and loss. People's relationships are so frail, and we are so uncertain as to how long we can have them. Learning that all we have are all temporary gifts from the Lord, and God is the only one who will be with us forever, will give us proper perspective.

So, don't let your children think that they own things or will have people forever. Time is passing and our life is short. If they don't learn that, they can fall into deep disappointment, discouragement, depression and despair when they lose someone or something they love.

Paul wrote, *"For, as I have often told you before and now say again even with tears, many live as enemies of the cross of Christ. Their destiny is destruction, their god is their stomach, and their glory is in their shame. Their mind is on earthly things. But our citizenship is in heaven. And we eagerly await a Savior from there, the Lord Jesus Christ."* *(Philippians 3:18-20)*

Teach children to look up to God when they are hurting from grief and loss. When they have faith in God, He will help them heal from grief and loss by helping them to have a proper perspective.

Prayer: "Lord Jesus, please help me to experience healing when I go through grief and loss. Help me to teach my children how to experience healing when they go through grief and loss as well."

15. Teach them how to forgive

Teach your children to forgive by showing them that you forgive them when they make a mistake. By treating them with gentleness and compassion when they make a mistake, you are teaching them how to forgive. This doesn't mean that you are letting them get away with something. You tell them what is right and wrong, then teach them that they can also be forgiven.

How can we teach our children to forgive? Again we have to be a good example; we need to share our feelings with our children to teach them how we learned to forgive. *"Do not judge, and you will not be judged. Do not condemn, and you will not be condemned. Forgive, and you will be forgiven." (Luke 6:37)*

My daughter developed an outstanding practice for disciplining her children. When her children fight, the one who did wrong has to go to their bed until they decide to come out and say sorry to the other siblings and give them a hug. This teaches them the consequences and responsibility without getting violent toward children or using harsh discipline.

Jesus told us to pray, bless and forgive others. We need to remind our children how to let go of anger, resentment, hate and bitterness, so they won't be consumed with negative feelings and fall into sin. Helping children to have faith will help them to learn how to forgive because forgiveness is what God wants. He will teach our children. Forgiveness is a decision we have to make to obey the Lord.

Adult children's comments:

"My faith helped me to forgive myself; to let the anger and the past go. It also caused me to worship and praise day and night, always giving glory to Jesus."

Prayer: "Lord Jesus, I forgive everyone who has sinned against me. Help me to provide an environment where my children can learn how to be gentle and have mercy when others make mistakes."

16. Protect them from violent situations

Many children who come from violent homes can become violent if they don't reflect and learn to resist their violent temper. We need to break the cycle. God can help us do that. If you are suffering from a violent temper, I ask you to ask the Lord to forgive you. Ask your family to forgive you and don't repeat the same mistake.

Many children are damaged because they grew up in fear and violence. Create peace in the family by restraining your own temper and don't justify your sin. Take parenting classes, anger management classes or get professional help if you cannot control yourself.

If you are living in a violent situation, you need to protect yourself and your children. Seek outside help and get advice on how to resolve the situation If that doesn't work, you may have to remove yourself and your children as soon as possible. There are many horror stories when people put up with violence in their home.

Adult children's comments:

"What I was lacking as a parent was that I let my kids see too many things that I didn't think they should see. I thought they didn't know what was going on. But every time their dad hit me and called me names, they had seen it. They ended up needing mental therapy for it. They started being violent as early as two years old. It affected me because I lost them, due to domestic violence. I let it happen for too long. I was scared to reach out. I wish I could have reached out for help instead of being in fear of being hurt. I got hurt anyway."

"My father molested me and it made me not know who to trust as for men."

"I wish my mother wouldn't have done drugs while pregnant with me or have given me to my step father to use at his sexual disposal. I hate her because I am so overly protective of my kids. I don't want anyone around them. I hated her, but I forgave her."

Prayer: "Lord Jesus, please help me to create a safe and peaceful environment for my children. Give me the wisdom to discern whom I can trust and whom I should stay away from. Help my children to be surrounded with godly people so they can grow in an environment of love and peace. Help me to be gentle, kind and compassionate toward everyone, especially to my children."

17. Teach them good moral values

Our culture has accepted immoral behavior as moral and normal behaviors such as sex outside of marriage. God has a high moral standard for our sexual behaviors but the worldly standard is following our own sinful desires.

This is a very difficult lesson for our children who grew up with TV and in a culture where having sex outside of marriage is normal. Sexual perversion is accepted as a normal practice even though it goes against the Scriptures. We need to teach our children God's standards over and over again. We need to teach our children about the responsibility to wait until they are married to have sex and will be able to take care of their children. When we are not ready to have children and are not able to take care of them, the children pay the price.

Adult children's comments:

"I wish that I would have waited until I was older to have children. I wasn't prepared as a mother mentally or emotionally. I was 15 years old and still a kid myself, not ready to be a parent, but the thing is I didn't even realize that I didn't know how to be a parent. I didn't have the skills. I didn't have a good role model for parenting. I wish I was mature enough not to fall into addiction or to come out of it faster. I would be more attentive and always show up for everything at school, watch them play sports etc. You have to keep kids busy and active."

Prayer: "Lord Jesus, help me to live a godly life and be a good example to my children in all areas. Help them to have a pure heart, clear conscience, strong faith and high moral values so they can resist temptation to an immoral lifestyle. Protect them from ungodly people and to live a godly life."

18. Be there for your children

Many adult children express that they wished their parents were there when they were growing up. Many of them expressed that not only physical presence is important but also truly being there for them emotionally.

Listen to them when they talk to you. This will help them to know that you care about them and that they are valued. When you don't listen and ignore them, they may stop talking to you. They will look for others with whom to share their feelings, and you could miss being involved in many things where you might make an impact on their life journey.

Adult children's comments:

"I wish my parents would not have neglected me when I was young. I now suffer from abandonment issues as a result of that. I grew up feeling unimportant and now I fight for attention by having extreme behaviors like sex, drugs, etc... seeking attention from all the wrong places and people. I was not taught a lot of basic things in life like doing laundry, cleaning, the facts of sex and how and why babies are created."

"My dad wasn't involved in my life. It affected me because I always blamed my mom for everything that went wrong. And I felt like my dad didn't care about me or love me. So in turn I told my mom it was all her fault and it started to take a toll on my relationship with her. I hated my dad and felt he hated me. He told me once he didn't want anything to do with me because he hated my mom and that hurt me. It's not my fault he didn't like her."

"I regret getting into the prison system. After my

divorce, my life just seemed to go down hill with alcohol and drugs. I was 33 years old when I went to jail and I have been in the system since. I had to leave my children which were in my custody at the time. This was in 1994 and my son was 11 and my daughter 6 when their dad had to take care of them. This was the start of not being there for them. I missed a lot of their growing teenage years and many holidays. To this day, I cry and it makes me sad."

"My father spent a lot of time with me. He changed his work schedule so that he could be my primary caregiver in the daytime while my mother worked then she took care of me in the evening. Looking back, I realize how much of a sacrifice they made to nurture me. I felt important, loved and my self-esteem was high."

"My mother worked too much and was never really home and that left me with my abusive step-dad."

Prayer: "Lord Jesus, help me to listen to my children so I can understand where they are. Let them see that I care and let them know that I am always there for them. Help me to spend more time with them so I can build up a loving relationship with them."

19. Teach them to pray

Teach your children how to pray and listen to God. Teach them the Lord's Prayer and explain to them the meaning of the prayer. Even if they don't understand, you can ask them to recite the Lord's Prayer when they are little so they can learn to pray. Remind them to learn to communicate with Jesus when they are hurting and when they are happy, so they can develop a relationship with Jesus.

Teach them to listen to God. Encourage them to wait and listen after they pray so they can give Jesus time to speak to them. Prayer is a communication between us and God. Encourage them to meditate, memorize and read the Bible, so they will know what are good thoughts and bad thoughts. If they are good thoughts or helping them to do good things, it is coming from the Lord. But if they are bad or negative thoughts, they need to resist them and turn to God for wisdom to resist them.

Before you put your children to bed take the opportunity to teach them how to pray. Ask them to think about what they can be thankful for and encourage them to tell God how thankful they are. Teach them to pray if they have nightmares. God can heal them from nightmares and give them strength.

Adult children's comments:

"My grandmother who helped raise me taught me about the power of the name of Jesus. I used to have many bad dreams. In my sleep I would call out in the name of Jesus. It would wake me up. I know how to pray and take authority in His name because she taught me this."

"Something I did with my own daughter and my step sons is before they would get out of the car to go to school, I prayed over them."

Prayer: "Lord, help me to teach my children to pray and learn how to recognize your voice. Bless them with the gift of faith. Help them to have the heart and desire to love you and serve you."

20. Lead them to the Lord

Many children who attend church are not saved if the church does not help them to realize they need to make the choice to accept Jesus. People can have Bible knowledge but never make a commitment to accept Jesus as their Savior. So, make sure that your children understand that they need to invite Jesus in order to have a relationship with Him. Jesus is knocking on the door of our hearts and we need to open our heart to invite him to have a relationship with him.

If you are a parent trying to teach your children about God, remember you need to have a relationship first so you can teach them how they can be saved. If you have not given your life to Christ or if you are not sure if you are saved or not, you can accept Jesus by inviting him into your heart. You can also help your children to invite Jesus into her/his heart by helping them recite the prayer to invite Jesus into their hearts if they cannot read. The following prayer is for you and for your children if you are not saved.

Prayer: "Lord Jesus, I believe in you. I give my life to you. Come into my heart and my life. Help me to have a loving and close relationship with you. I believe you died for my sins and you were raised from the dead. I ask for your forgiveness for my sins. Please teach me how to love you and serve you. In Jesus' name I pray. Amen."

"For God so loved the world that he gave his one and only Son, that whoever believes in him shall not perish but have eternal life." (John 3:16) *"That if you confess with your mouth, 'Jesus is Lord,' and believe in your heart that God raised him from the dead, you will be saved. For it is with your heart that you believe and are justified, and it is with your mouth that you confess and are saved."* (Romans 10:9-10)

21. Be their cheerleader

Always believe in your kids and be their cheerleader. Work on having a close relationships with your children, even when their behavior is not acceptable. They are in the process of growing, and no one is perfect. Let them know your standards and values, but also communicate that you love them, so they can come to you when they are in trouble and need your advice or your help. Tell them how proud of them you are, so they know you value them.

Being a cheerleader is being positive in every situation so your children will know that you are for them, even when discouraging events happens. We need to help our children by building up their confidence so that they know they are worth something in this world; that their contributions would make a difference. We need to constantly tell our children how proud we are. Make them understand that their presence brings us joy. When we can convince them that we are for them and they are important to us, we can gain their confidence in us as parents as well.

Adult children's comments:
"My mom stayed consistent in telling me to keep pushing forward through hard times and not to give up. This affected me in a positive way because I'm still here pushing forward as hard as ever to get through this tough time of being incarcerated, away from my child."

"My dad was always my superman and still is. He always listened to me. Just as my mother had. They both spoke great lecturing skills to me when I did wrong. And that helped me to see that I was very loved."

"My parents had great hearts and that gave us great love. All my grandkids and kids were given great love too and they had much respect for each other."

"My parents loved me and made me feel special. They taught me how to love and make my son feel special."

Prayer: "Lord Jesus, with your wisdom, help me so I can always be a cheerleader for my children. Help me so that I can also help my children with the kind of love you have for me. Thank you for the gift of my children."

22. Teach them to love God more than money
We need to teach our children how important it is to obey the Lord. It's a good practice to give to others who are less fortunate than us. Giving teaches us how to be humble because we cannot take anything with us when we die. Sometimes we think and act like this world is where we will live forever; but giving and sharing teaches us we are here

temporarily. Everything is the Lord's and we don't own it. If we can understand that God is the owner of everything, and how He wants to teach us how to be generous with what He gives us, we will be able to let go of our selfishness.

"For the love of money is a root of all kinds of evil. Some people, eager for money, have wandered from the faith and pierced themselves with many grief's. But you, man of God, flee from all this, and pursue righteousness, godliness, faith, love, endurance and gentleness. Fight the good fight of the faith. Take hold of the eternal life to which you were called when you made your good confession in the presence of many witnesses." (1 Timothy 6:10-12)

Prayer: "Lord Jesus, teach me how to serve you with what I have so I can teach my children that they need to love and serve you, not material things or money."

23. Teach them to have a dream

We need to teach our children that the Lord has plans for them. We also need to communicate to them that we believe in them. Try to provide the best opportunities for them to excel in school and anything that is good for them, especially serving the Lord by serving others. Provide all your children's basic needs and love so they can go beyond survival mode but use their creativity and dreams to help others. *"'For I know the plans I have for you,' declares the LORD, 'plans to prosper you and not to harm you, plans to give you hope and a future.'"* (Jeremiah 29:11)

Prayer: "Lord Jesus, please bless me with the wisdom to understand your visions, dreams and plans for my life and help me to obey you. I also pray for all my children to understand your visions, dreams and plans for them and that they will have the heart to obey you."

24. Dedicate your children and find peace

Hannah dedicated Samuel even before he was conceived. I encourage you to dedicate your children to the

Lord and pray for them. Dedication does not mean that they will become ministers but that you are asking the Lord to guide and direct your children's life as He wants. Many parents are in anguish when their children take the destructive path. We let go of our control and let God control their lives. Pray for them and give them to the Lord when you start worrying about your children and are filled with fear.

Prayer: "Lord Jesus, I give you my children for your work for the rest of their lives. Bless them with faith and love for you and love for themselves and others. I thank you for taking care of my children. Amen."

25. Ask God for help with parenting

God is not only interested in your well-being but your children's well-being as well. He wants to help you so that you can help your children to grow in faith. That's why the Lord told the Israelites to teach their children about God.

Read the Bible and pray regularly and focus on your spiritual growth so you can help your children to grow spiritually. You cannot give what you don't have. Attend church to show your children that you need God; that you need His wisdom in all areas so they can learn to rely on the Lord. Ask God for wisdom so you can avoid making mistakes that you will regret. Learn from your parents' mistakes and don't repeat them. Also, when your children are following the worldly, destructive, sinful, path, ask the Lord to help you with wisdom to help them, as well as what to say to them.

Prayer: "Lord Jesus, help me to have wisdom to say the right things to my children when they follow a sinful path so they can repent and turn to you."

26. Ask for forgiveness when you make a mistake

If you have made a mistake or hurt them, ask your

children to forgive you. In this way, they don't have to suffer from resentment, anger and bitterness. Help them to develop good character by being a good example. Don't go to the grave without asking your children to forgive you if you hurt them in any way.

Prayer: "Lord Jesus, help me so when I hurt my children, I can recognize it and ask them for forgiveness. I pray they will not hold resentment or anger against me."

27. Encourage them to get a higher education

Children with a higher education have a better chance of succeeding in life. Encourage your children to get a higher education when they are little. When they try to make decisions, encourage them as much as you can so they will pursue a higher education. People who have more education earn more and they have less chance of being stricken by poverty. When we are successful, we can be more generous to others who are needy. Encourage your children to be their best and fulfill their dreams by achieving a higher education. Ask them to ask for God's wisdom and teach them a good study habits. Reward them when they do well.

Prayer: "Lord Jesus, help me to encourage my children to be the best they can be; and to learn as much as they can so that they can be used by you to help many others who are in need of transformation. Please surround our children with people with goals of helping others so they can learn to follow you and bring transformation in the world."

28. Find godly mentors for your children

You need to find some mature Christians who can help you to be better parents. Also, your children need godly mentors who can help them with God's values. Ask the Lord to help you find a mentor for your children. Ask your pastor or other mature Christians if they know anyone who could mentor your children.

Prayer: "Lord Jesus, help my children to have Christian, godly mentors. Protect my children from ungodly people. Help me to find good godly mentors for my children."

29. Encourage them to read good books

What your children read will affect their mind and lives. There are many good books that could help your children to grow; the Bible is one of them. There are also many other books inspired by many godly people who wrote them to help others. Make a list of the books that you think are good books, help them to read and reward them. Take them to the library at an early age so they can learn to love to read. I actually paid my children to read when I felt the book was worthwhile to read. We didn't give them allowances so that motivated them to read more.

Prayer: "Lord Jesus, I need your wisdom to know which books can help my children to grow in faith and live a godly life that will please you. Please help me to help my children to be inspired by other godly people who wrote to change the hearts of people, the community, and the world. Help me to teach the Bible to my children, so they can understand how much you love them."

30. Don't repeat the mistakes your parents have made

Are you still grieving over your parents' mistakes? You need to learn the lessons and not repeat the same mistakes. Spend time writing the lessons you have learned from your parents, good or bad. Then make plans as to how you are going to act differently. Find out what you need to do to forgive, to let your anger and resentment go so you can teach your children what you have learned.

Prayer: "Lord Jesus, help me to learn the lessons from my parents, so I will not repeat their mistakes."

31. Have a good relationship with your spouse

Many children feel insecure and live in fear if their parents do not have a good relationship. If you have problems with your spouse, try to read the Bible and pray together. Ask the Lord to give you wisdom to solve the problems with God's help. Forgive each other and learn to process your pain so you can provide a loving, nurturing and peaceful environment for your children. You might need to seek pastoral counseling or a marriage counselor if you cannot solve the marriage problems, but reading the Bible and praying together is a good start. I believe some divorces could be avoided if you seek God's advice; then a couple could learn to forgive, love and respect each other.

Except with some abusive situations, most of the time divorce can devastate children. Many children do not handle their parents' break ups well. It could be the point at which children start acting out and turn to a destructive path. So, if you can, work on your relationship with your spouse, not only for you and your spouse, but for your children's well being.

Adult children's comments:

"I wish my parents had a good marriage and were happy with each other. It made me feel unimportant because they were too busy fighting with each other. I could never have any friends come over because I never knew when they would break out arguing. It created shame. I was embarrassed when my friends came over and they would fight, yell, and scream. I felt shame to have to make excuses why my house is not a good house, why we would have to go to someone else's house."

"I wish my parents had togetherness and would not argue but pay attention to me."

Prayer: "Lord Jesus, I need your wisdom so I can have a good, loving relationship with my spouse. Please help me to find a way to create peace and love with your help so I can help my children to grow up in a loving and nurturing environment to teach them about your love and your greatness."

32. Teach them to listen to God's voice

Do you know that God can speak to us through the Words from the Bible and dreams? He also speaks to us with a small voice in our minds by guiding and warning us about different matters. God has given us a great gift, the Holy Spirit, to guide our path to a peaceful and godly life. Many people who have ignored the small voice made wrong decisions. They ended up grieving and hurting themselves and others.

Teach your children to pay attention to the small voice which will guide them to do good. Encourage your children to read the Bible and ask God for wisdom to make the right decisions when they are confused or face challenging situations. Whenever they have uneasy feelings about something, the Holy Spirit may be warning them not to take the wrong path and that they need to pay attention. When your children face problems, pray with them for the Holy Spirit's guidance so they can learn to pray and ask for guidance in their early age.

Adult children's comments:
"Father God helped me to know I was worth a lot. He talks to me throughout my life, showing me how to handle things and what to say or what not to say. God continues to give me dreams and a message that shows He loves me and it makes me strong."

Prayer: "Holy Spirit, please bless my children with an open heart, so they can seek your guidance and recognize your voice and they will follow the righteous path."

33. Teach them about the spiritual battle

Not only can the Holy Spirit speak to our heart, but the devil can speak to our mind and try to plant destructive thoughts and attitudes. We need to teach our children the reality of the spiritual battle going on in our minds, so they can learn to resist the critical, judgmental, and destructive voices which will lead them to temptation and sin. We all have a good character that God has given us, but we also have a sinful nature which plays a big role in creating turmoil. The devil tries hard to bring discord. If people do not pay attention to what they hear in their mind, sometimes they may follow the destructive voices without realizing that that is from the enemy the devil.

When your children are acting out, there is a chance that they have not learned to resist the destructive suggestions that come into their minds. I heard many who committed crimes and fell into sin heard voices telling them what to do. They didn't realize that it was the devil's voice. They followed the voices and got into deep trouble. Our ignorance and sinful nature plays a role in our life but many times the destructive voices and thoughts we hear have the origins of the devil.

Here is a warning. When your children are acting out, don't tell them that they are the devil or they are acting out like a devil. Don't tell them that Jesus wouldn't love them if they act bad. They are not the devil and they are not acting like a devil but they may not have the discernment to know what is right or wrong. Also, Jesus has more compassion and understanding than us parents. Let's not make them feel Jesus is condemning them. Teach them to resist the negative voices by replacing them with Bible verses. We all make mistakes out of ignorance or a rebellious heart. The worst mistake is to make your children feel that they are bad because of your critical attitudes, words and actions.

Prayer: "Lord Jesus, help me to have the wisdom to

The Ultimate Parenting Guide

teach my children how to listen to your words so they can find peace. Surround them with angels and protect them."

34. Teach them to love and worship Jesus

Teach them the importance of worshipping Jesus everyday, not just at the church. Start praising Jesus on all occasions. Make time to worship Jesus at home so your children can learn to love Jesus. This will be a good foundation for relationship. Worship Jesus throughout the day and invite Him to be the leader of your home. Did you know that you can find joy when you worship Jesus? If you teach your children to praise Jesus all the time, you will be blessing them with spiritual strength in times of trouble or even in good times.

Prayer: "Lord Jesus, help me to worship you everyday and every moment. Help my children to do the same, so I can help them to look up to you and recognize your great love and power in our lives. I love you, help me to love you more. Help me to teach my children to love you everyday."

35. Teach them to find a spouse with high moral values

People with low morals think other people are disposable and don't have any commitment in relationships. So, marriage wouldn't last because the focus is not to make his spouse or family happy but only their selfish desires and lustful passion. We need to teach our children to stay away from these people or they will get hurt.

Lots of breakups in marriages are caused by people who do not have any respect or regard for anyone but themselves. They have no fear of God when they sin and have no fear of hurting others. If your children don't know how to discern and recognize other people's value system, they may end up marrying someone that has low moral values and end up getting hurt.

A beautiful woman was lamenting how her ex-husband was deeply in love with her before they got married. After they had been married about 15 years, this man fell in love with another woman and left his wife. This woman didn't understand why he left. I told her that this man didn't have high moral values and followed his own sinful, selfish desires and worldly passion, instead of keeping his vows of marriage. Every one will face temptations, but how we choose to resist them and to live a godly life is based on our values and moral standards.

Adult children's comments:

"My mother was weak willed regarding men and needing love. I did not see a godly relationship between a man and woman. I did not understand how to be a wife or how I should respect myself with men."

"My mother chose a wicked and dangerous man to marry. She lacked good judgment. Her father begged her not to marry him and her husband later beat my grandfather with a hammer."

Prayer: "Lord Jesus, help me to teach my children how to find good spouses who love God and have high moral values so they can live a peaceful life of love."

36. Learn the lessons from Job about parenting

We can learn about parenting from Job. He was a praying man, he prayed for his children. When he lost everything including all his children - seven sons and three daughters, and all his possession - he didn't lose his faith.

The Scripture tells us, "*At this, Job got up and tore his robe and shaved his head. Then he fell to the ground in worship and said: 'Naked I came from my mother's womb, and naked I will depart. The LORD gave and the LORD has taken away; may the name of the LORD be praised.' In all this, Job did not sin by charging God with wrongdoing.*" (Job 1:20-22)

Our life, our possessions and all we have including

The Ultimate Parenting Guide

our children are temporary gifts from the Lord. Job understood this. His focus was not his loss but to worship God. Our physical bodies have limitations and eventually we all die. No one lives forever, but our spirit lives forever. We need to love God more than our children or possessions. That's what Job was doing. Job is a great example for us to follow.

Prayer: "Lord Jesus, thank you for my children. Please bless me with understanding that all my gifts are temporary gifts and they all belong to you. I give everything to you, especially my children. Please guide and direct me so I can help my children with the gift of faith and the knowledge that all we have is yours and everything is a temporary gift."

37. Teach them about humor and coping skills

Life can be hard if we don't know how to cope with hard times. Sometimes our children can get hurt because they take things too seriously. Teach them how to let go of others' rejection or harsh treatment by not taking it so seriously, but give everything to the Lord, and let it go.

Teach them how to laugh it off when things get tough. Humor can be a life saver in a stressful situation when it is used in the right place and at the right time, it will lighten the load of what we carry. Find a time to teach them how to laugh and enjoy life. You might purchase a book of humor if you need some creative stories.

Prayer: "Lord Jesus, help me to have creativity so I can teach my children how to cope with life's struggles with humor and your joy. Bless our family with joy and laughter."

38. Teach them to be self-sufficient

Teach your children to clean their rooms and teach them do their own laundry when they are big enough to take care of themselves. Our children were given the responsibility of doing their own laundry when they were ten years old. We told them when they were little that they would start doing their own laundry when they turned ten. Since then they have been taking care of their own laundry. It worked out very well, not only did our children learn to take care of themselves but it also gave them confidence. Also, encourage them to find a job when they can work, so they learn to develop good work ethics and learn to appreciate what they have.

There may be some children who have mental or physical disabilities and may not be able to do this so you need to know how much your children can take on.

Prayer: "Lord Jesus, please help me to prepare my children to be self-sufficient, so they can take care of themselves and gain confidence in what they can do to take care of themselves."

39. Take them on trips to build good memories

Make plans to go on a trip and help your children to have good memories of spending time with you. Teach them to enjoy the beauty of nature. Introduce them to other places and people where you can teach them to have a broader perspective. When they are little, take them to the play ground and parks so they can learn to have fun time with you. This will help them to have positive memories of you and will help build a better relationship. It will also help you to have good memories about your children as well.

Prayer: "Lord Jesus, teach me how to be creative so my children can have good memories of spending time with me."

40. Proclaim victory for your children

When you face difficulties or are filled with fear and worry because of your children, pray for miracles and proclaim victory in Christ. Here my prayer of victory and you can write your own:

A victory prayer for my children

I claim victory that my children will be saved by God's grace.
I claim victory that God will take care of my children for His glory.
I claim victory that my children will be filled with the Holy Spirit and serve God to the fullest.
I claim victory that God will give my children spiritual blessings beyond their imagination.
I claim victory for my children that God will provide what they need, including godly mentors.
I claim victory that my children will be blessed with spiritual gifts and use them for God's glory.
I claim victory that God will take care of my children when I cannot take care of them.
I claim victory that God will protect my children and help them grow in faith.
I claim victory that other people will be blessed by my children's presence and ministry.

Chapter 5

An Invitation

1. An Invitation to Accept Christ

Do you have an empty heart that cannot be filled with anyone or anything? God can fill your empty heart with His love and forgiveness. Do you feel your life has no meaning, no direction, no purpose, like you don't know where to turn to find the answers? It's time to turn to God. That's the only way you can understand the meaning and the purpose of your life. You will find direction that will lead you to fulfillment and joy. Is your heart broken and hurting, and you don't know how to experience healing? Until we meet Christ in our hearts, we cannot find the peace and healing that God can provide. Jesus can help heal your broken heart. If you don't have a relationship with Christ, this is an opportunity for you to accept Jesus into your heart so you can be saved, find peace and healing from God. Here is a prayer if you are ready to accept Jesus.

"Dear Jesus, I surrender my life and everything to you. I give you all my pain, fear, regret, resentment, anger, worry, and concerns that overwhelm me. I am a sinner. I need your forgiveness. Please come into my heart and my life; forgive all my sins. I believe that you died for my sins and that you have plans for my life. Please heal my broken heart and bless me with your peace and joy. Help me to cleanse my life so I can live a godly life. Help me to understand your plans for my life and help me to obey you. Fill me with the Holy Spirit, and guide me so I can follow your way. I pray this in Jesus' name. Amen."

2. An Invitation for The Transformation Project Prison Ministry (TPPM).

Chaplain Yong Hui V. McDonald has been in prison ministry since 1999. She started working as a chaplain at the Adams County Detention Facility (ACDF) in Brighton, Colorado, in 2003. She started the Transformation Project Prison Ministry (TPPM) in 2005 in an effort to bring spiritually nurturing books to the inmates at the facility. In the process, *Maximum Saints* books and DVDs were produced by ACDF inmates for the other inmates.

The *Maximum Saints* books and DVDs project provides the ACDF incarcerated saints an opportunity, and offers encouragement to put their writing and artistic skills to use to provide hope, peace, restoration, and healing. It gives spiritual support to incarcerated people, the homeless, as well as to interested persons outside the prisons.

Maximum Saints are not necessarily classified as maximum security inmates; they are called Maximum Saints because they are using their gifts to the maximum to help others.

TPPM produces books and DVDs are distributed free of charge in jails, prisons and homeless shelters nationwide. As of 2010, TPPM has published eight English books, two Spanish books, produced four DVDs, and distributed more than 100,000 free copies of books and DVDs to prisons and homeless shelters.

"One Million Dream Project"

America has 2.3 million people incarcerated, the largest prison population in the world, and there is a great shortage of inspirational books in many jails and prisons.

In 2010, TPPM board decided to expand the ministry goal and started, "One Million Dream Project." TPPM decided to raise enough funds to distribute one million copies of each book that TPPM has produced for prisoners and homeless people. Please pray for this project so we can reach out to those who cannot speak for themselves, but are in need of spiritual guidance from the Lord.

TPPM is a 501(c)(3) nonprofit organization so your donation is 100% tax deductible. If you would like to be a partner in this very important mission of bringing transformation through the message of Christ in prisons and homeless shelters or want to know more about this project, please visit: www.transformprisons.org.

You can donate on line or you can write a check addressed to: Transformation Project Prison Ministry and send it to the following address:

Transformation Project Prison Ministry
5209 Montview Boulevard
Denver, CO 80207

Phone: 720-951-2629
Website: www.transformprisons.org
Email: transf@gbgmchurches.gbgm-umc.org
Facebook: http://tinyurl.com/yhhcp5g

ABOUT THE AUTHOR

Yong Hui V. McDonald, also known as Vescinda McDonald, is a chaplain at Adams County Detention Facility, certified American Correctional Chaplain, spiritual director, author, and on-call hospital chaplain. She founded the Transformation Project Prison Ministry (TPPM) in 2005 and founded GriefPathway Ventures LLC in 2010 to help others learn how to process grief and healing.

Education:
- Multnomah Bible College, B.A.B.E. (1984)
- Iliff School of Theology, Master of Divinity (2002)
- The Samaritan Counseling & Educational Center, Clinical Pastoral Education (CPE) (2002)
- Rocky Mountain Pastoral Care and Training Center (CPE) (2003)
- Formation Program for Spiritual Directors (2004)

Books Written by Yong Hui V. McDonald:
- *Moment by Moment*
- *Journey With Jesus, Visions, Dreams, Meditations & Reflections*
- *Dancing in the Sky, A Story of Hope for Grieving Hearts*
- *Twisted Logic, The Shadow of Suicide*
- *Twisted Logic, The Window of Depression*
- *Dreams & Interpretations, Healing from Nightmares*
- *I Was The Mountain, In Search of Faith & Revival*
- *The Ultimate Parenting Guide, How to Enjoy Peaceful Parenting and Joyful Children*
- *Prisoners Victory Parade, Stories Behind Maximum Saints Book and Former Prisoners' Transformations*
- Compiled and published five *Maximum Saints* books under the Transformation Project Prison Ministry.

DVDs produced by Yong Hui V. McDonald:
- Two *Maximum Saints* DVDs
- *Dancing in The Sky, Mismatched Shoes*
- *Tears of The Dragonfly, Suicide and Suicide Prevention*

Spanish books:
- *Twisted Logic, The Shadow of Suicide*
- *Journey With Jesus, Visions, Dreams, Meditations & Reflections*

Audio Books:
- *Journey With Jesus*
- *Dancing in the Sky, The Story of Hope for Grieving Hearts*
- *Twisted Logic, The Shadow of Suicide*
- *Twisted Logic, The Window of Depression*
- *Dreams & Interpretations, Healing from Nightmares*
- *I Was The Mountain, In Search of Faith & Revival*
- *The Ultimate Parenting Guide, How to Enjoy Peaceful Parenting and Joyful Children*
- *Prisoners Victory Parade, Stories behind Maximum Saints books and Former Prisoners' Transformations*
- *Tears of the Dragonfly, Suicide and Suicide Prevention*

GriefPathway Ventures LLC
P.O. Box 220
Brighton, CO 80601

Website: www.griefpathway.com.
Email: griefpwv@gmail.com